Fighter Bases of World War II – 8th Air Force USAAF 1943–45

P-47 Lightning, P-38 Thunderbolt & P-51 Mustang Squadrons in East Anglia, Cambridgeshire and Northamptonshire

Fighter Bases of World War II – 8th Air Force USAAF 1943–45

P-47 Lightning, P-38 Thunderbolt & P-51 Mustang Squadrons in East Anglia, Cambridgeshire and Northamptonshire

Martin Bowman

First published in Great Britain in 2009 by
Pen & Sword Aviation
An imprint of Pen & Sword Books Ltd
47 Church Street
Barnsley
South Yorkshire
S70 2AS

ISBN 978 1 84415 905 5

A CIP catalogue record for this book is
available from the British Library

Typeset in 10pt Palatino by Mac Style, Beverley, East Yorkshire
Printed and bound in the UK
By CPI

Pen & Sword Books Ltd incorporates the Imprints of Pen
& Sword Aviation, Pen & Sword Maritime, Pen & Sword
Military, Wharncliffe Local History, Pen & Sword Select, Pen
& Sword Military Classics, Leo Cooper, Remember When,
Seaforth Publishing and Frontline Publishing

For a complete list of Pen & Sword titles please contact
PEN & SWORD BOOKS LIMITED
47 Church Street, Barnsley, South Yorkshire, S70 2AS, England
E-mail: enquiries@pen-and-sword.co.uk
Website: www.pen-and-sword.co.uk

Contents

Acknowledgements

Patty Bauchman; Theo Boiten; Tony Chardella; David and Lorinda Crow; Tom Cushing; Bill Espie; Michael Fuenfer; Richard E. Flagg; Steve Gotts; Steve Graham 669 Squadron Army Air Corps (AAC); Alan Hague; Andy Height; Lieutenant Colonel R. A. 'Dick' Hewitt; Imperial War Museum (IWM) Duxford; Pete Keillor; Walt Konantz; Ian McLachlan, Nigel McTeer; Larry Nelson; Merle C. Olmsted; Colonel Ernie Russell; the staff of the 2nd Air Division Memorial Library, Norwich: Buzz Took; Roy West; Paul Wilson.

Introduction

It is due entirely to the long-range escort fighter that even when B-17 and B-24 losses reached epidemic proportions from late 1943 to spring 1945 the 8th never abandoned its daylight precision bombing concept in the European Theater of Operations (ETO). Range was not something that had influenced the equipment of fighter units destined for England because it was thought that operations would be similar to those undertaken by RAF fighters where high-altitude performance seemed to be the important factor. The 8th Air Force had begun the bomber offensive from East Anglia in 1942 with the steadfast belief that compact bomber formations could fight their way

In December 1942 the 78th Fighter Group arrived in England with P-38 Lightnings but re-equipped with the P-47 in late January 1943. Ultimately, four American fighter groups – the 20th, 55th, 364th and 479th – equipped with P-38H and J Lightnings flew combat missions from England. (USAF)

Ground crew working on an overturned P-47 Thunderbolt. (USAF)

unescorted to a target in the face of fighter opposition and still strike with acceptable losses. In late 1942, all but one of the 8th Air Force's Fighter Groups (4th Fighter Group) were sent to North Africa. In December the 78th Fighter Group arrived in England with P-38 Lightnings. The fastest American fighter available when war began, the P-38 was the first twin-engine, single-seat fighter ever mass-produced. Ultimately, four American fighter groups – the 20th, 55th, 364th and 479th – equipped with P-38H and J Lightnings flew combat missions from England until replacement by the P-51 Mustang in July–September 1944. The Mustang, ironically, had resulted after a visit made by the British Purchasing Commission officials to America in April 1940. Meanwhile, a decision was made to re-equip both the 4th and 78th Fighter Groups with P-47 Thunderbolts and VIIIth Fighter Command began 1943 with three P-47 groups following the arrival of the 56th Fighter Group. By year-end the number had risen to ten. The 8th Air Force planned on using the P-47 force to support its daylight bomber operations and the pilots were first to gain operational experience under the tutelage of RAF Fighter Command. Spitfires had been employed in offensive cross-Channel operations since spring 1941 mostly on 'Rodeos' whereby several squadrons carried out a high speed sweep over France or the Low Countries to lure enemy fighters into combat.

A young Dutch family with a 108-gal drop-tank, which was dropped by a P-47 over Zuid-Scharwoude, northern Holland on 29 May 1944 when 187 Thunderbolts flew escort and support for the heavies attacking aircraft plants and oil installations. (Ab A. Jansen via Theo Boiten)

However, the *Luftwaffe* often refused to rise to take the bait and so a 'Circus' consisting of a small number of bombers with very strong fighter support was despatched. A fighter escort for a true bomber operation was known as a 'Ramrod'.

When planning P-47 missions the prime consideration in 1943 was range, or rather the lack of it. Early P-47 missions without belly tanks averaged 1 hour and 45 minutes to the maximum of 2 hours and 5 minutes. Increasing use of bigger and better drop tanks enabled the P-47 Groups to fly operations up to 5 hours and 30 minutes and fighter units were assigned their escort relay points by the size of the tanks they carried on the operation, which dictated their range. On 4 May VIII Bomber Command dispatched seventy-nine B-17s on a five-hour round trip to the Ford and General Motors plants at Antwerp. They were protected by twelve Allied fighter squadrons, including for the first time by six squadrons of P-47 Thunderbolts of the 4th and 56th Fighter Groups who provided fighter escort up to 175 miles. In four hours VIIIth Bomber Command attacked four targets, losing twelve B-17s and B-24s and claiming sixty-seven fighters shot down. RAF Spitfires and USAAF Thunderbolts had given excellent fighter cover on the Antwerp and Courtrai raids.

On 17 August 1943 four P-47 groups were scheduled to escort the Regensburg force but only the two squadrons in the 353rd Fighter Group (later relieved by the 56th Fighter Group) rendezvoused with the bombers as scheduled but their task was impossible. The overburdened Thunderbolts could not possibly hope to protect all seven B-17 groups in a long straggling formation that stretched for 15 miles. Fortresses in the rear of the formation were left without protection at all and VIIIth Bomber Command lost thirty-six Fortresses on the Schweinfurt raid with a further twenty-four being lost on the Regensburg strike, making sixty lost in combat.

During the bloody aerial battles of late 1943 unescorted bombers penetrated deeper into Reich airspace than ever before and over sixty heavies were lost on a single mission. Single-engine fighters such as the nimble Spitfire and P-47 Thunderbolt, an aircraft double the weight of a Bf 109 and half

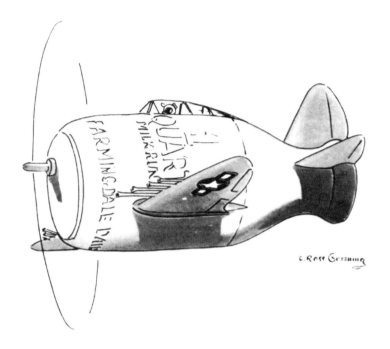

'The Flying Milk Bottle', otherwise known as a P-47 Thunderbolt, by Colonel
Ross Greening.

as much again as the Fw 190, had only enough range to escort
the bombers part of the way and to meet them on their return.
After the heavy losses on the second Schweinfurt raid on 15
October desperate US attempts were made to improve fighter
cover. The P-38 had good escort range but it was usually second
best in combat with the Bf 109 and Fw 190. Eaker knew that
deep penetration missions were finished unless a proven long-
range escort fighter could be found. "At this point nothing was
more critical than the early arrival of the P-38s and P-51s", he
said. The P-51B Mustang was not only capable of meeting the
Bf 109s and Fw 190s on even or better terms; it could escort the
B-24s and B-17s to their targets and back again. The Mustang's
range of 2,080 miles was far in excess of that available in other

fighters of the day and this was achieved by the internal fuel it carried.

In November 1943 the first deliveries of P-51Bs were to three groups of the tactical 9th Air Force at the expense of 8th Fighter Command, whose need was critical. The first escort mission for the bombers was finally flown on 5 December. On the 13th, when in a record flight, 649 bombers bombed naval targets at Bremen, Hamburg and Kiel, P-51s reached the limit of their escort range for the first time. On 10 February 1944 the long-ranging P-51s could accompany the heavies to their targets and back again but they were powerless to prevent German fighters destroying twenty-nine of the 169 Fortresses despatched. Next day the first P-51Bs joined VIII Fighter Command when the 357th Fighter Group at Raydon, Essex received them. They flew their first escort mission next day. During 'Big Week' (20–25 February) 8th and 15th Air Force bombers and 1,000 fighters were despatched almost daily on the deepest penetrations into Germany thus far. On 6 March 730 B-17s and B-24s and 801 P-38, P-47 and P-51 escort fighters were despatched to targets in the suburbs of Berlin in the first American air raid on Big-B. Eleven fighters were lost, while 102 bombers were seriously damaged. In March P-51Bs flew to Berlin and back for the first time.

Near the end of 1943 when returning home from escort missions P-47s began strafing targets of opportunity on the ground and it proved so successful that the P-47D was adapted to carry wing mounted bombs to add to the destructive power of its 6 or 8 inch machine guns. On 11 February 1944 when the first P-51s joined VIII Fighter Command, the bombers were protected by 15 groups of escorting fighters who helped keep bomber losses to just five. On 25 February when the USSTAF brought the curtain down on 'Big Week' 1,300 8th and 15th Air Force bombers and 1,000 fighters were despatched on the deepest penetration into Germany thus far and the fighters claimed eighty-one enemy fighters destroyed. The late February to early March period of 1944 was the Thunderbolt's heyday as far as air fighting went. Thereafter the *Luftwaffe* would be more difficult to encounter and the Mustang's advantage of greater endurance than the P-47s saw them regularly running up substantial scores as the P-51 saw

DUTIES OF A FIGHTER PILOT

ESCORT MISSION.

ESCORT MISSION
(WITH BELLY TANKS)

Cartoon 'Duties of a Fighter Pilot'.

widespread use as an escort fighter on long-penetration raids deep into Germany. The Mustang had the lowest fuel consumption of the three main USAAF fighters, the P-51B using 65 gallons per hour (gph) and the P-47D more than double this at 140gph. The P-51 equipped all but one of the 8th Air Force Fighter Groups and the majority of Thunderbolts were used to equip the 9th and 15th Air Forces in England and Italy respectively for fighter-bomber operations. By June 1944 thirteen P-47 groups of the IXth and XIX Tactical Air Commands in southern England were equipped with the P-47D Thunderbolt to support the coming cross-Channel invasion and once bases had been established, move to the continent as soon as airstrips had been built by IX Engineer Command.

On D-Day 6 June the Allied air forces numbered over 4,100 fighters of which 2,300 were USAAF day fighters and 1,890 fighters of all types by the RAF. In response the *Luftwaffe* had only 425 fighters of all types in Normandy of which only 250–280 were serviceable on any one day. Escort numbers rose steadily mission by mission and from September 1944 on, all but one of the 8th Fighter Groups flew P-51s. On 28 July 1944 over 700 B-17s were protected by 437 fighters, which later broke away to strafe ground targets. Seven B-17s and two P-51s were lost. On 11 August, 578 fighters escorted 956 heavy bombers and two days later six fighter groups escorted over 1,300 heavy bombers. On 26 August 956 bombers were protected by 897 fighters and on 10 September over 1,000 bombers were escorted by several hundred fighters in attacks on targets in Germany. Next day fourteen fighter groups were airborne as six synthetic oil plants and other targets in Germany were hit. The missions were flown in the face of an estimated 525 enemy fighters and fifty-two heavies and thirty-two fighters were lost. On 9 October over 1,000 heavies bombed targets in western Germany escorted by nineteen fighter groups including two in the 9th Air Force which provided support. Two days later 130 B-17s supported by three P-47 groups bombed targets at Wesseling and Koblenz. On the 12th eleven fighter groups escorted the bombers and claimed eighteen enemy fighters shot down. On 22 October more than 1,000 heavies supported by fifteen fighter groups attacked war plants at Brunswick and Hanover and marshalling yards at Hamm and at Münster. On 24 October, 415 P-47s and P-51s of the 8th Air Force carried out fighter-bomber raids in the Hanover-Kassel area. Nine aircraft were lost. Next day almost 1,200 heavies in five forces supported by eleven fighter groups attacked three oil refineries and several other targets. It was the same on 26 October, when over 1100 heavies attacked an oil plant at Bottrop and several other targets supported by fourteen fighter groups. The pattern was the same in November with up to eighteen fighter groups supporting the bombers on each series of raids every day they were flown. On 2 November the Mustangs routed their German attackers and the 352nd Fighter Group established a record thirty-eight kills on that occasion.

The *Luftwaffe* though was far from defeated and production of fighter aircraft actually increased in 1944 and into 1945. It had peaked in September 1944 when an astonishing 1,874 Bf 109s and 1,002 Fw 190s were completed. That same month, an average of three German fighters and two pilots KIA were

P-51s undergoing maintenance at the Base Air Depot at Burtonwood. (USAF)

lost for every B-17 or B-24 shot down. The USSTAF was clearly winning the battle of attrition in the conflict with the *Luftwaffe*, which was forced on the defensive and irreparable harm was caused by shortages of pilots, aircraft and fuel. American Fighter Groups never suffered the same shortages.

December 1944 brought the worst winter weather in England for 54 years but the fighter groups provided support for the bombers when the conditions allowed, during the Battle of the Bulge. It culminated on 23 December when a dozen VIIIth Air Force fighter groups supported 400 B-17s and B-24s which hit lines of communication behind the Ardennes area to offer some hope to the hard-pressed infantry divisions in the 'Bulge'. Nearly eighty enemy fighters were shot down.

January 1945 marked the VIIIth's third year of operations and it seemed as if the end of the war was in sight. However, *Unternehmen Bodenplatte*, a desperate gamble to diminish the overwhelming Allied air superiority, was mounted on New Years Day using 875 single-engined fighter aircraft, primarily in support of von Rundstedt's Ardennes offensive. But though total Allied aircraft losses amounted to 424 destroyed or heavily damaged the *Luftwaffe* lost 300 aircraft, 235 pilots killed and 65 pilots taken prisoner.

On 14 January when fifteen fighter groups were airborne 161 enemy aircraft were destroyed for the loss of only thirteen P-51s and three Thunderbolts. The *Wehrmacht* advance in the Ardennes had ultimately petered out. In the east the Red Army prepared for the great winter offensive, which would see the capture of Warsaw and Krakow and take the Soviets across the German border. Hitler's last chance now lay in his so-called 'wonder weapons'; the V-1 and V-2. Final victory, though never in doubt, was hard fought and drawn out by a dogged defence, especially when the Allies advanced into Germany. Ever diminishing numbers of *Luftwaffe* fighters, which kept rising to attack, were mostly destroyed by the P-51s and P-47s. On 17 April more than 950 B-17s and B-24s attacked eight railway centres, junctions, stations and marshalling yards and an oil depot in east Germany and western Czechoslovakia. Eighteen US fighter groups flew support, encountering about fifty fighters, mostly jets and claimed thirteen destroyed including four jets. The American fighters strafed numerous airfields and claimed over 250 aircraft destroyed on the ground. Eight B-17s and seventeen fighters were shot down. The last major air battles between fighter groups of the 8th Air Force and the *Luftwaffe* took place on 18 April when over 1,200 heavies escorted by more than 1,200 fighters attacked Berlin. Forty Me 262s shot down twenty-five bombers with rockets. It was the final challenge by a dying enemy. The *Luftwaffe* was finished, destroyed in the air and starved of fuel on the ground.

The Airfields

Atcham (Station 342)
Atcham in far-flung Shropshire was taken over by the USAAF in June 1942 as a base for the operational training of fighter pilots. Initially, Spitfires and Miles Masters were operated and later P-47s were primarily used, although, late in 1943, some P-38s were used. On Christmas Day 1943 the 495th Fighter Training Group was formed with two squadrons of P-47s and conducted a finishing school for both the Eighth and Ninth Air Forces. When training replacement fighter pilots was switched to the combat groups, Atcham was gradually run down. So too was the satellite airfield at High Ercall, which was handed back to the RAF in 1943. Atcham was returned to the RAF on 14 March 1945 and became a satellite of RAF Ternhill in Flying Training Command.

Bodney (Station 141)
In the summer of 1943 this RAF satellite grass airfield with a macadam-surfaced perimeter track was turned over to the USAAF. The technical area was on the western side and twenty-six tarmac hard-standings were dispersed in woodland bordering the airfield. Domestic sites were in two groups north and south-east of the airfield. On 8 July the 352nd Fighter Group, which was equipped with P-47D Thunderbolts, was established at the airfield although some of the personnel had to be quartered temporarily at RAF Watton until work on the Nissen hut sites was finished. Steel matting was also laid and pierced-steel planking hard-standings were built and additional tarmac taxiways and roads were built as the heavy Thunderbolts turned the grass into a quagmire in the winter months. The 352nd began flying combat missions on 9 September 1943. In March–April 1944 the group converted to the P-51B Mustang.

Captain Virgil Kersh 'Virg' Meroney back from another successful mission. The five kills chalked up on the nose of P-47D-5-RE 42-8473 'Sweet Louise' made him the first ace in the 352nd Fighter Group at Bodney. (USAF)

They became famous throughout the Eighth as the 'Blue Nosed Bastards of Bodney'. In all, the Group flew 420 missions in WWII and lost 118 fighters in action while claiming 519½ enemy aircraft destroyed in the air and 287 on the ground.

On 30 December 1943 the 352nd Fighter Group's P-47s, which were scheduled to cover the withdrawal of the bombers failed to show. Things had begun to go wrong almost from the outset. Colonel Joe Mason, who was leading his Group, encountered a solid overcast but he continued on course. Because of their contrails the Bomber withdrawal track could be seen a long way ahead and Mason also saw that the first two boxes of B-24s were under P-47 escort. Mason turned his Group back along the bomber track and picked up two boxes of B-17s flying about 15 miles to the rear and 15 miles starboard of the first boxes seen. Nothing was seen to the rear of the bombers. Escort was given to these two boxes and several stragglers flying with them. The 352nd Fighter Group left them at 1400 hours and headed toward home base.

As the 352nd continued on into France and approached Chalons, several pilots in the 328th Fighter Squadron noted a sharkmouthed Me-110 flying parallel to the bombers and attacked it. Within minutes the plane went down under the combined fire of Lieutenant Colonel Eugene 'Pop' Clark and Lieutenants William Hendrian and Dave Zimms. A short time later, as they neared the port city of Calais, three Fw 190s attacked the 487th Fighter Squadron and this interception set in motion the events, which cost the squadron three of its most experienced pilots. The 4th *Staffel* JG 26 had taken off from Wevelgem to look for stragglers near Dunkirk and they found a flight of three Thunderbolts, which were too low on fuel to stay and fight. They had dropped their belly tanks early in the mission when a Bf 109 was sighted and the additional drain on their fuel with the escort assignment lasting nearly 10 minutes longer than scheduled. This left them little choice, when they were bounced, but to try to evade the 190s by diving away. *Fähnenjunker-Feldwebel* Gerd Wiegand chased Captain Don Dilling out to sea and later claimed to have shot him down but out of fuel he belly landed in a field. Dilling evaded and eventually returned to England via Spain. Flak batteries at Dunkirk claimed Captains Hayes Button and Winfield McIntyre but they too had run out of fuel and they came down in enemy territory.

On 4 February during combat with the 352nd and 56th Fighter Groups JG 26 lost one of its pilots and three others were wounded in action. 'The Blue Nosed Bastards' had rendezvoused with the bombers, which were far off course, in the vicinity of Aldenhoven. During the first 40 minutes of the escort all was quiet but as the formation arrived in the vicinity of Brussels

Lieutenant Virgil K. Meroney at wing root of P-47D-5-RE 42-8473 'Sweet Louise' on 26 September 1943. (via Bill Espie)

the 328th Squadron noticed two separate formations of bandits. One gaggle of Fw 190s was at 26,000ft near Brussels and the second was near Hasselt at 15,000ft. During the engagements that followed Lieutenants Francis Home and Fremont Miller each claimed an Fw 190 destroyed. Lieutenant Virgil Meroney fired at an Fw 190 at 200 yards and watched as the enemy aircraft (e/a) burst into flames but two P-47s and their pilots were killed in the vicinity of Emden. Lieutenant Ray Cornick in the 328th Fighter Squadron was shot down and Flight Officer Joseph Sweeney in the 487th ran out of fuel on the return trip and is believed to have crashed in the Channel.

On 8 February 1944 JG 26 pilots also shot down six P-47s and P-51s in the 352nd and 354th Fighter Groups. Immediately after rendezvous with the bombers, Red Flight of the 328th Squadron were *en route* to assist a straggling B-17 being attacked by an Fw 190 when they came under attack from *Hauptmann* Karl Borris and his 1st *Staffel* formation. They bounced them from out of the sun and shot down two P-47s. North of Laon *Leutnant*

Ground crew's side of P-47D-5-RE 42-8473 'Sweet Louise' in the 352nd Fighter Group with the names 'Miss Josephine' and 'Hedy' being the wives of Staff Sergeant Al Giesting and Sergeant Jack Gillenwater. (via Bill Espie)

Waldemar 'Waldi' Radener claimed two more of the Group's P-47s. One of his victims crashed but Lieutenant Raymond Phillips reached England and bellied his P-47 in on the coast.

On 8 March 1944 the 352nd was one of the groups that provided withdrawal support for bombers returning from 'Big B'. Cloud covered England as the 'Bluenosers' took off from Bodney. Before the mixed formation of seven P-51s and sixteen Thunderbolts could clear the overcast, six of the P-47s in the 486th Squadron were involved in mid-air collisions. The rest of the Group continued to the rendezvous point (RP) near Weitzen without seeing any enemy fighters. By the time the 352nd arrived for withdrawal support the fighting had subsided but near Dummer Lake Captain Edward J. 'Pappy' Gignac, leading Purple Flight of the 486th Squadron in P-51 Mustang *'Little Rebel'* saw a straggling B-17 under attack by a Bf 109. Gignac immediately called a bounce and started down. The 109 got several hits on the B-17 before Pappy could reach it. As he closed, he broke off his attack with a violent aileron roll and pulled up into a vertical climb. Gignac reefed it in violently and took a short burst but his closing speed was so high that he could not follow him up. Even though his burst was short and

Lieutenant Colonel John C. Meyer, CO, 487th Fighter Squadron in the cockpit of 'Petie 2nd' at Bodney. Meyer destroyed twenty-four enemy aircraft in the air (and two half shares) 1943–45, as well as thirteen on the ground. (via Bill Espie)

at great deflection Pappy Gignac claimed destruction of the 109 because Lieutenant Ed Heller, flying Green 2, saw the pilot bale out just after he fired at him and saw the aircraft hit the ground and explode. Gignac's victory was the first of many the 352nd Fighter Group would score in the P-51 Mustangs.

About 10 minutes later over Meppen as the 487th was being relieved of escort duty by another unit three Bf 109G-6s of JG 26 broke out of the sun. Captain Virgil Kersh 'Virg' Meroney

P-51D 44-14151 'Petie 2nd' in the 487th Fighter Squadron at Bodney. (USAF)

who was leading Blue Flight in P-47D 42-8473 '*Sweet Louise*' called out a warning to the Squadron and then led his Flight in pursuit. Meroney, who had six outright victories and two half shares, picked out the leader of the enemy formation. Two other Mustang pilots got on the tail of his wingman, *Unteroffizier* Emil Kempen of 9./JG26 who was shot down and killed at the Steinhuder Lake west of Hanover. The leader tried to go to the aid of his wingman but he was hit and damaged by Meroney with a burst of fire at high deflection. The German broke away and Meroney followed his quarry down to treetop level and overtook him. As he pulled up on the Messerschmitt's right wing the pilot jettisoned his canopy. Meroney was sitting right on his wing and got a good look at him. Though he did not know it at the time, his victim was Major Klaus Mietusch who was flying a Bf 109G-6. Mietusch's parachute opened immediately and he landed safely but his injuries were severe enough to keep him in hospital for a short spell. Meroney's 8th victory firmly established him as the 'Bluenosers' scoring leader and foremost P-47 Ace. Meroney scored a 9th and final victory on 16 March before he was shot down by flak and taken prisoner on 8 April 1944.

Major George E. Preddy, whose final confirmed score of 26.833 (and 5 strafing) victories made him the second highest scoring American fighter ace in the ETO behind Gabby Gabreski. (USAF)

On 11 April the 352nd Fighter Group was split into two formations, one comprising the P-51 equipped 486th and 487th Fighter Squadrons to provide penetration support for the B-17s of the 1st Air Division and the second comprising the 328th Fighter Squadron providing withdrawal support for the bombers. The Blue Nosed Bastards joined with the bombers near Stendal. The 40 minutes of escort was uneventful but as the P-51s broke off escort they were immediately presented with a number of ground targets. The 486th strafed two airfields near Torgau and claimed three aerial victories, seven more destroyed on the ground and two Ju-86s probably destroyed and four others damaged in ground attacks. First Lieutenant Frank A. Cutler who was leading Blue Flight in 'Soldier's Vote' strafed some planes on an airfield at Nehmsdorf and he damaged a Ju 52 three-engined transport. Cutler then took his flight to a field a few miles to the west near Lonnewitz where he saw a number of white Ju 88s and he got good hits all over the wings and engines of one and left it burning. Leaving this field Cutler was flying in a westerly direction when he saw a locomotive just leaving the bridge across the Elbe River at Torgau. Cutler made his pass at the engine and saw pieces of it thrown up in the cloud of steam from the boiler. He then flew over the town of Torgau on the rooftops heading west for a mile or two. He was keen to add to the two Bf 109s he had scored over Belgium on 20 February when he had been flying a P-47 and near Neiden-Torgau Cutler got his chance. When he looked to the left and behind he saw a Ju 52 and closed on him fast to about 200 yards before pulling the trigger. There were strikes on the landing gear and left wing root. As he passed over him Cutler flipped over and saw the

Having dispensed with his 75-gallon 'teardrop' tanks to give him optimum manoeuvrability at low-level, Lieutenant Karl Dittmer of the 487th Fighter Squadron taxies out at Asch (Y-29), Belgium in mid-January 1945 in 'Dopey Okie' to commence yet another short-range patrol over the slowly advancing Allied frontline. Dittmer had claimed one kill up to this point in his career in the ETO. (via Bill Espie)

left wing and engine in flames and his wingman saw it hit the ground and burn. As he was on his back heading north and watching the Ju 52 go down Cutler saw two light blue Fw 190s flying wingtip to wingtip directly below going west at about 1,000ft. *Unteroffiziers* Heinz Voight and Karl Weiss of 4/JG 26 were flying them. Cutler headed for them, closed fast and shot both of them down. Cutler's claim for the Ju 52 destroyed in the air was reduced to a half share after gun-camera film showed that Anderson had also fired on the fighter and scored hits. Cutler received credit for the destruction of the two Fw 190s as well as one Ju 88 destroyed and one Ju 52 damaged on the ground and one locomotive destroyed. Cutler destroyed two Bf 109s on 8 May and he destroyed another Bf 109 on 13 May to take his score to 7.5. He was killed in a collision on 13 May.

In the early hours of D-Day, 6 June 1944 during take-off four abreast in poor visibility in the dark with 'oil-drum lighting' Lieutenant Bob Frascotti in *'Umbriago'* flew into the new,

P-51B and D Mustangs of the 487th Fighter Squadron, 352nd Fighter Group at Bodney, Norfolk. Nearest Mustang is 44-13530 'Millie'. A 12 inch blue cowling band was introduced in April 1944 and extended back covering the black anti-dazzle panel to the cockpit that same month. (via Bill Espie)

incomplete control tower and was killed instantly. It was his 89th mission. One Mustang had the volley-ball net wrapped around the wing leading edge. The control tower was repaired and still stands today though the old tower has long since gone. In late June US Secretary for War, Henry Stimson, visited the base during his visit to the UK.

Flight Lieutenant Edwin H. King RAF who was seconded to the 487th Fighter Squadron, recalls:

On 5 August we were to escort the bombers 'Ramrod 483', to the target area (Magdeburg) joining up with them as they coasted in at Den Helder which meant getting to height over the UK. One could hear the bombers climbing whilst we were still at briefing and since the weather was poor we had to climb in sections through cloud from 600 to 18,000ft, joining up as a squadron and then a group on top. Over the continent the cloud began to break up and there was considerable opposition almost all the way in. I was again No.2 to Major Preddy and watched him get two Me 109s. I only got a squirt at one. After the target we were relieved and returned direct to UK with no further action, just the usual flak.

Preddy was awarded confirmation of one Bf 109 destroyed and one probable. Next day he shot down six confirmed Bf 109s before going on leave until October 1944. He returned as CO, 328th Fighter Squadron.

On 23 September 1944 during a support mission for 'Market Garden' the 352nd Fighter Group suffered their greatest single mission loss to date. The 'Bluenosers' lost a P-51 to flak near Gennep and 45 minutes later a disaster befell the 487th Squadron when all four Mustangs in Red Flight were shot down at about 1,500ft when they were bounced by a superior force of German fighters. Then they were fired at from the ground so the P-51s dropped down to about 500ft. They started to circle and still had their drop tanks on. They were spotted just under the cloud cover and eight to ten Fw 190s opened fire. One of the pilots was Captain Clarence O. Johnson, who had destroyed four and claimed three probables flying P-38s in the MTO and claimed three in the air and six more on the ground during his tour with the 487th, giving him a grand total of thirteen destroyed, three probably destroyed and one damaged. At the time of his death Johnson was among the top ten in 352nd scoring and was thirteenth at war's end.

The 352nd was awarded two Distinguished Unit Citations, for the mission on 8 May 1944 when escorting B-17s on the raid on Brunswick and the other, for the 487th Fighter Squadron only, for the destruction of twenty-three enemy aircraft on 1 January 1945. The 487th was the only squadron in the 8th Air Force to receive independently a Distinguished Unit Citation (DUC). The 352nd destroyed thirty-eight enemy aircraft in a fight on 2 November 1944. Major George E. Preddy (twenty-five) had the highest score of any Eighth Air Force Mustang ace. On 25 December 1944 Preddy scored his two final victories to take his score to 26.8333. He was killed by friendly fire the same day. His 20-year old brother William was lost on a mission with the 339th Fighter Group at Fowlmere.

Part of the 352nd Fighter Group moved to Asche in Belgium just before Christmas 1944 to help counter the threat posed by von Rundstedt's offensive in the Ardennes. In early April 1945 the 352nd returned from the continent to fly the remainder of its wartime missions from Bodney. The group left for the USA in early November and Bodney airfield reverted to farmland. The airfield is on the northern extremity of the 20,000-acre Stanford Battle Training Area and one of the original accommodation sites, south of the B1108, is a British Army Camp.

Bottisham (Station 374)
Bottisham airfield was constructed as an auxiliary field during the early years of the war for use by RAF Army-Co-operation aircraft of 168 Squadron flying Mustangs. It was then enlarged during the winter of 1943–44. Areas of steel matting were laid on the airfield prior to the arrival in November 1943 of the 361st Fighter Group, the last Thunderbolt group to join the Eighth. The steel matting supported the heavy P-47 Thunderbolt fighters but the landing strip was unsuitable for wet weather operations and in three days during January 1944 American engineers built a 1,470-yard-long runway with pierced-steel planking. This was considered to be a record for laying this type of prefabricated surfacing. The runway, which was aligned NE-SW, became the

P-51Ds of the 374th Fighter Squadron, 361st Fighter Group overflying an airfield. Nearest aircraft is B7-W 44-14305. (via Steve Gotts)

main runway, the other also being constructed of PSP. In May 1944 the Group converted to the P-51 Mustang, its aircraft being given yellow spinners and nose bands, which earned the Group its nickname, the 'Yellowjackets'. During the pre D-Day rail

Bottisham, 31 August 1944. P-5ID 'Gentle Annie' was flown in by Colonel Harold Rau, CO 20th Fighter Group; 'Straw Boss 2' PE-X 44-14111 by Lieutenant Colonel James Mayden, CO 352nd Fighter Group; P-47D-25-RE 42-26641 LM-S 'Hairless Joe' by Colonel Dave C. Schilling, CO 56th Fighter Group 12 August 1944–27 January 1945 (42-26641 was the aircraft in which Schilling destroyed five enemy aircraft on 23 December 1944); P-51D 44-14291 CL-P Da Quake by Colonel John L. 'Jarring John' McGlinn, CO 55th Fighter Group; P-47 Judy by Colonel Phil Tukey, CO 356th Fighter Group; P-47D LH-E, by Colonel Ben Rimmerman (KIFA 11 August 1945), CO 353rd Fighter Group and P-38J (right) by Colonel Hub Zemke, CO 479th Fighter Group 12 August-30 October 1944, when he was taken prisoner. (USAF)

374th Fighter Squadron, 361st Fighter Group P-51B and D Mustangs from Bottisham photographed from a 91st Bomb Group B-17 on 11 July 1944. Nearest aircraft is P-51B 42-106839 B7-E 'Bald Eagle' flown by Robert T. Eckfeldt. Next is P-51D 44-13357 B7-R 'Tika IV' flown by Lieutenant Vernon Richards, then B7-O 44-13857 and P-51B B7-H. On 25 June 1944 Richards shot down an Fw 190 and a Bf 109 in rapid succession. (via Tom Cushing)

P-51D 44-13926 E2-S being flown by 1st Lieutenant Urban Drew in the 375th Fighter Squadron. E2-S has been hastily sprayed with OD paint when VIIIth FC thought it would have to forward deploy fighters to France soon after D-Day and it was almost brand new when this shot was taken on 11 July 1944. Later assigned to Lieutenant Abe P. Rosenberger, 44-13926 was written-off in a crash on 9 August whilst being flown by Lieutenant Don Dellinger, who was killed. (via Steve Gotts)

375th Fighter Squadron, 361st Fighter Group P-51B and D Mustangs from Bottisham on 11 July 1944. The Group CO, Colonel Thomas J. J. Christian is leading the four-ship in P-51D 44-13410 E2-C 'Lou IV IV/Athlene'. Christian was shot down and killed on 12 August 1944 in this Mustang. The second P-51D in the formation is 44-13926 E2-S, being flown by the Group's third-ranking ace, 1st Lieutenant Urban Drew. Alongside Drew is Lieutenant Bruce Rowlett in his personal Mustang, 44-13568 E2-A 'Sky Bouncer', whilst occupying the No.4 slot in soon to be retired P-51B 42-106811 E2-H 'Suzy G' is Captain Francis Glanker. (via Steve Gotts)

interdiction programme the Group was credited with destroying twenty-three locomotives and damaging two others.

On 8 April 1944 the 'Yellowjackets', which were being led by Colonel Thomas J. Christian Jnr, the first commanding officer of the 361st Fighter Group, flew their most successful mission to date. They claimed nine aircraft destroyed, two probables and two damaged for the loss of one pilot. One of the victories went to First Lieutenant Alton B. Snyder who pumped 750 rounds into the Fw 190 flown by Leutnant Karl 'Charlie' Willius, 2./JG26 CO, who was killed near Genemuiden, Holland. (His widow Lisette received a posthumous *RitterKreuz* [RK or Knight's Cross] on 9 June 1944. Willius' body was not recovered until 1967, buried in his Fw 190 15ft deep in a Dutch polder). The use of the 150 gallon

P-51D 'Mountaineer' in the 363rd Fighter Squadron, 357th Fighter Group after crashing at Bottisham. (USAF)

1st Lieutenant William Rockafeller Beyer, known as 'Bright Eyes' by his squadron buddies and well liked by everyone, had gained his first victory in the 376th Fighter Squadron, 361st Fighter Group on 17 September when he shot down and killed Major Klaus Mietusch, CO, III./JG 26, a career officer who was a veteran of 452 combat sorties and had claimed seventy-two aerial victories. (via Steve Gotts)

Lieutenant Colonel Wallace E. Hopkins of the 361st Fighter Group on the wing of P-51D 44-13704 B7-H 'Ferocious Frankie' at Bottisham, his second Mustang named for his wife. Hopkins was flying this aircraft when he shot down two Fw 190s on 8 August 1944 to take his final wartime score to four. He was Group Operations Officer and he flew seventy-six combat missions. (USAF)

Lieutenant Vernon D. Richards in the 374th Fighter Squadron, 361st Fighter Group. (USAF)

First Lieutenant (later Major) Urban L Drew, 375th Fighter Squadron, 361st Fighter Group who finished his combat tour with six confirmed victories. On 7 October 1944 flying P-51D 44-14164 'Detroit Miss', Drew shot down two Me 262s of Kommando Nowotny *over Achmer airfield, the first Allied fighter pilot to down two of the jets in one sortie. Upon his return the American ace was recommended for the award of the DSC, but was turned down because of insufficient information. Drew's camera-gun had jammed and his wingman, Lieutenant Robert K. McCandliss, had broken away during the attack to avoid flak and had not witnessed the actual shootdowns (McCandliss was shot down over Rheine airfield and became a PoW). In 1967 Drew received confirmation of the two victories from none other than Major Georg-Peter Eder, who witnessed everything from the ground after aborting his take-off with engine failure! In May 1983 Ben Drew was presented with the award of the Air Force Cross (modern equivalent of the DSC and ranked second only to the MoH). He and Eder, two former adversaries, became firm friends. (via Steve Gotts)*

drop tank had boosted combat endurance by a wide margin but the P-47's capacity for burning fuel, especially in the high rpm settings necessary in a dogfight, was unsurpassed and many pilots returned to Bottisham 'on vapours'. Christian, who became CO of the 361st Fighter Group on 13 February 1943 when it was activated at Richmond AAB, Virginia, was killed in action when leading the group on a mission over northern France on 12 August 1944. Light flak brought down his Mustang 'Lou IV' when he was dive-bombing rail targets at Arras, France. Three other Mustangs

1st Lieutenant William 'Bill' Rockafeller Beyer (left) with 1st Lieutenant Victor Bocquin (right) who was leading the 376th Squadron, who together accounted for 8 e/a destroyed are writing up their encounter reports after their combat on 17 September 1944. After interrogation Intelligence personnel confirmed that the 376th Fighter Squadron's claim of 18 aerial victories plus three ground claims amounted to a record total for any 8th Air Force squadron in a single day's operations. (via Steve Gotts)

in the 361st were also lost. On 17 September during the prelude to 'Market Garden' the Group was among those who tussled with JG26 in the mid-afternoon on this momentous day. For four pilots killed in action JG26 claimed three of the 'Yellowjackets' in the Mönchengladbach and Nijmegen areas. JG26's greatest loss was 25-year old Major Klaus Mietusch, CO, III./JG26 who was shot down and killed by 21-year-old First Lieutenant William R. Beyer in the 376th Fighter Squadron. Mietusch was a veteran of 452 combat sorties and he had claimed seventy-two aerial victories. Beyer later recalled:

The Me 109 I followed used every evasive action to lose me, flying through clouds and doing several 'split-esses' between 15,000ft and the deck. He chopped his throttle and threw

Second Lieutenant William R. Beyer (left) posing for a PR photo with Captain Roy Webb. On 27 September Bill Beyer destroyed no less than five Fw 190s in the vicinity of Eisenach. In total Beyer scored nine confirmed wartime victories by 26 November 1944. (via Steve Gotts)

down flaps at 1,000ft and did another 'split-ess'. I did the same and got on his tail on the deck. I began firing at 200 yards using about 40° deflection and got a few hits around the cockpit. He tried to continue his turn but went straight on into the ground, the pilot apparently dead.

In all, the pilots of the 375th and 376th Squadrons claimed fourteen enemy aircraft destroyed, giving the 361st the day's highest total of planes shot down in the 8th Air Force. Among those who recorded aerial victories was Second Lieutenant Claire P. Chennault in the 376th Squadron, whose father, the legendary Major General Claire Chennault, had led the famous American Volunteer Group ('The Flying Tigers') in China before the US entered the war.

Operating from St. Dizier, France on 26 December 1944 1st Lieutenant George R. Vanden Heuvel in the 376th Fighter Squadron, 361st Fighter Group, shot down an Fw 190D-9 flown by Oberleutnant Hans Hartigs of the 4th Staffel JG 26. (via Steve Gotts)

On 26 December 1944 2nd Lieutenant. Claire P. Chennault in the 376th Squadron, 361st Fighter Group, claimed an Fw 190D of the 4th Staffel JG 26 destroyed. Chennault's father, the legendary Major General Claire Chennault, had led the famous American Volunteer Group ('The Flying Tigers') in China before the US entered the war. (via Steve Gotts)

On 26 September 1944 the 361st Fighter Group moved to Little Walden, which offered an improvement over Bottisham's rustic conditions. In all, the 'Yellowjackets' flew 441 missions and lost eighty-one aircraft in action, claiming 226 enemy aircraft destroyed in the air and 105 on the ground.

Boxted (Langham) (Station 150)

Boxted airfield was built by W. & C. French Ltd almost entirely in the village of Langham as a heavy bomber base to the standard Air Ministry Directorate General Works (AMDGW) design, but it was given the name Boxted, an adjoining village, to avoid confusion with Langham airfield in north Norfolk. Boxted's main SW-NE runway was 2,000 yards long and the two intersecting runways were 1,400 yards each in length. There were fifty hardstandings and two T2 type hangars were constructed, one on the south and one on the west side of the airfield. Accommodation was provided for 2,900 personnel and all temporary buildings were dispersed in fields and woods to the south of the airfield. Boxted airfield was ready for flying by late May 1943. A B-17 group, which was scheduled for June went to Norfolk and instead, on 12 June, Boxted received the 386th Bomb Group equipped with B-26B/C Marauders and

P-51B of the 355th Fighter Squadron, 354th Fighter Group, the pioneer Mustang group, which was assigned to the 9th AF, flying its first mission on 1 December 1943, but which operated under 8th AF control for almost the first six months of its combat career. (USAF)

P-47D-25-RE 42-26628 'Miss Fire Rozzie' Geth II LM-C, flown by Captain Fred J. Christensen, of the 62nd Fighter Squadron. The aircraft was named after Christensen's girlfriend, Rosamund Gethro. He scored his 14th victory (a Bf 109) in this Thunderbolt on 27 June 1944, and his 15th (an Fw 190) on 5 July. Two days later flying another P-47D, he took his total for the war to 21½ (ten of which had been scored in the first 'Rozzie Geth') by shooting down six Ju 52s. (Bill Cameron)

P-47C-5-RE 41-6584 'Holy Joe' was flown by 26-year-old 1st Lieutenant Joe L. Egan Jr of the 63rd Fighter Squadron. Joe had only been Squadron CO for two days when, on 19 July 1944, he was shot down and killed by flak north-east of Nancy France. With five confirmed victories, Egan had been awarded three DFCs and three Air Medals by the time of his death. (USAF)

Lieutenant Colonel Francis S. 'Gabby' Gabreski, CO, 61st Fighter Squadron. (USAF)

commanded by Colonel Lester Maitland. The first of two night attacks on Boxted airfield took place on 17 August 1943, when one man was killed and several were injured when bombs fell amongst some Nissen huts. In September, the 386th Bomb Group moved to Great Dunmow.

Construction work at Boxted finished in late 1943 when the airfield was turned over to the 354th Fighter Group, the first to be equipped with the P-51 Mustang. Although it was a Ninth Air Force group, the 354th came under the control of Eighth Fighter Command and provided long-range escort for 8th Air Force B-17s and B-24s. During December 1943 Lieutenant Colonel Don

61st Fighter Squadron armourers Sergeant John A. Koval (left) and Sergeant Joe DiFranze (right) rearming 'Gabby' Gabreski's P-47D-25-RE HV-A 42-26418. (USAF)

Blakeslee, CO of the 4th Fighter Group, was assigned to the 354th Fighter Group to help them enter combat. He was so impressed with the Mustang that when he returned to Debden he argued forcefully to be equipped with the Mustang, which they were at the end of February 1944. Blakeslee's total victory score was 14.5, seven of which were scored flying P-51B/D aircraft.

On 5 July 1944 Lieutenant Colonel Francis S. 'Gabby' Gabreski, CO, 61st Fighter Squadron, scored his twenty-eighth fighter victory of the war. Gabby was shot down on 20 July by flak at Bassenheim airfield and he was captured. (USAF)

On 11 January 1944 the Mustang was still a well-kept secret and the 354th Fighter Group in the 9th Air Force was the pioneer Mustang group in the ETO. Major James H. Howard, ex-Flying Tigers P-40 pilot in China and now CO of 356th Squadron, displayed 'conspicuous gallantry and intrepidity above and beyond the call of duty in action', with the enemy near Oschersleben when he came to the rescue of some Fortresses. Howard was flying his usual P-51B, '*Ding Hao!*' (Chinese for 'very good') when the 354th provided support for a formation

C.Ross Greening
1944

Portrait of Lieutenant Colonel Francis S. 'Gabby' Gabreski by Colonel Ross Greening in Stalag Luft I.

of B-17s on a long-range mission deep into enemy territory. As the P-51s met the bombers in the target area numerous rocket-firing Bf 110 *Zerstorer* fighters attacked the bomber force. The 354th engaged and Howard destroyed one of the 110s but in the fight lost contact with the rest of his group. He immediately returned to the level of the bomber formation and saw that the B-17s of the 401st Bomb Group were being heavily attacked by German fighters and that no 'little friends' were on hand. Howard dived into the formation of more than thirty German

L-R: Colonel Hub Zemke, Major Dave C. Schilling, Major 'Gabby' Gabreski and Captain Fred J. Christensen of the 56th Fighter Group at Boxted. (USAF)

fighters and for 30 minutes single-handedly pressed home a series of determined attacks. He shot down two more fighters and probably destroyed another and damaged one other. Toward the end of his action, Howard continued to fight on with one remaining machine-gun and his fuel supply dangerously low. Major Howard's brave single-handed action undoubtedly saved the formation. He was awarded the Medal of Honor, the only one ever awarded to a fighter pilot flying from England. Howard's total score was 8.333 – all except two victories being escorted flying the Mustang, 20 December 1943–8 April 1945.

In mid-April 1944, the 354th flew south to an airstrip in Kent before to moving to the Continent after the invasion of Normandy. Boxted in turn received the 56th Fighter Group from Halesworth, the 'Wolfpack' being commanded by Colonel Hubert Zemke. On D-Day Robert J. Rankin in the 61st Fighter Squadron was one who 'beat up everything' he could see, including an airfield where seven aircraft were lined up. The

Lieutenant Colonel 'Gabby' Gabreski of the 61st Fighter Squadron, taxiing in P-47D-25-RE HV-A 42-26418, which shows all twenty-eight of his aerial victories below the cockpit. (USAF)

56th Fighter Group had developed a new strafing technique, which entailed diving instead of coming in level. This made the P-47s harder to hit. When they got down to about 3,000ft they started to pull out of the dive and open up with their eight .50-calibre guns at the same time. As the noses of the P-47s swung in the pull out, the guns swept the field. The sitting planes were 'plastered'. Later Rankin and his colleagues ran into some Mustangs strafing a convoy of about twenty-five trucks and the P-47s joined in. Some of the trucks carried fuel and some munitions. When the thunderbolts made their first pass they had to circle around waiting for another. So many of the fighters were attacking the convoy that they had to queue up for a turn. The enemy crews ran for cover as the fuel went up and the munitions exploded. The flaming petrol spread over the ground under the trucks and a great column of black smoke billowed up.

While at Boxted Lieutenant Colonel Francis Gabreski destroyed his twenty-eighth enemy aircraft in air combat, making him the highest scoring American fighter pilot in Europe in WWII. On 20 July 1944, Gabreski force landed in enemy territory while strafing Bassenheim airfield near Koblenz and he was taken prisoner after evading capture for five days.

Lieutenant Colonel Francis S. 'Gabby' Gabreski, CO, 61st Fighter Squadron. (USAF)

On 21 September, during 'Market-Garden' ninety P-47s of the 56th and 353rd Fighter Groups provided escort and patrol support for the airborne forces. The 56th Fighter Group claimed twelve enemy fighters destroyed for the loss of one Thunderbolt but they could not prevent the 1st *Gruppe* JG 26 from claiming seventeen to twenty RAF C-47 Dakotas.

One of the 56th Fighter Group's greatest days at Boxted was on 23 December 1944 during the Battle of the Bulge. Nearly eighty enemy fighters were shot down and the 56th Fighter Group returned to Boxted having claimed the lion's share with thirty-seven destroyed, (later reduced to thirty-two on the evidence of gun camera film) one probably destroyed and sixteen damaged. Eight of the fifty-six P-47s despatched had returned early with mechanical and equipment problems leaving the remaining Thunderbolts to continue their sweep in the Bonn and Koblenz areas. Hostile forces were reported north of Bonn but the enemy fighters disappeared among the clouds. Dave Schilling's formation was vectored towards two other formations of about forty-plus Bf 109s and 60-plus Fw 190s. The 56th Fighter Group was flying at between 23,500 and 25,000ft, which gave them a 1,000–2,000ft height advantage over the enemy. Schilling directed his 62nd Squadron to spread out so that they might be mistaken for a *Luftwaffe* formation joining up, as their approach was being made from the rear. This tactic proved successful and the Thunderbolt pilots gained complete surprise. In the air battle that ensued Schilling shot down five enemy aircraft and the other pilots claimed fourteen. Major Harold E. 'Bunny' Comstock, 63rd Fighter Squadron CO, who was nearing the end of his second tour, led his formation against the Fw 190s and they claimed thirteen of the enemy. Comstock claimed two Fw 190s destroyed and two Fw 190s damaged SW of Bonn.

The 5th Emergency Rescue Squadron equipped with P-47D Thunderbolts for Air Sea Rescue was formed at Boxted in May

P-47 Thunderbolts in the 56th Fighter Group line up for take off from Boxted. (USAF)

46

1944. A single blister hangar was erected for the Air Sea Rescue Squadron, which occupied a dispersal area at the northern end of the airfield, which used a farmhouse as its administrative and headquarters building. The 5th ERS moved to Halesworth in January 1945. Late that same year, Boxted was taken over by the RAF and was used by Mosquito night fighters and in 1946 by 234 Meteor jet squadron. By the end of that year, the flying units had moved on and work had begun on resurfacing the main runway. However in view of its proximity to Colchester, over which the main runway approached, the Air Ministry decided to abandon plans to make Boxted a permanent fighter station and the work was never completed. It was closed on 9 August 1947.

Debden (Station 356)
W. & C. French Ltd built this famous Battle of Britain fighter station during the RAF Expansion Period, 1935–39. It had permanent brick barracks and administration buildings, three 152ft-span, C-type hangars adjacent to the technical site on the eastern side of the grass aerodrome. The station opened on 22 April 1937 for 1,700 personnel, mostly in the permanent buildings adjoining the technical and administrative site, with a few new sites located in temporary buildings in the vicinity. In 1940, two intersecting concrete runways and extensions to the taxiways and a Bellman hangar were added. Some of the early, Macadamed hardstandings had earth and brick blast walls surrounding them for protection. In turn, eleven blister hangars were erected at various points around the aerodrome. During the Battle of Britain, Debden airfield was a sector station in 11 Group, with eight RAF fighter squadrons being stationed here at different times. In 1941 American pilots flew from Debden with 52 OTU, which was established during February and August. From May 1942 No. 71 Eagle Squadron at Martlesham Heath in the Debden sector was a part of the Debden Wing taking part in on cross-channel operations. On 29 September 1942 the three Spitfire-equipped Eagle Squadrons were turned over to the US authorities, becoming the 4th Fighter Group (renumbered 334, 335 and 336 Squadrons). The event was marked by an official

Former 71 Squadron RAF Eagle pilot Major Henry L. 'Hank' Mills who joined the 4th Fighter Group at Debden on 23 October 1942. On 6 March 1944 Mills, who was the 334th Fighter Squadron CO, was shot down near Berlin and taken prisoner. He had six victories. (USAF)

ceremony on the parade ground attended by Air Chief-Marshal Sir Sholto Douglas and Major General Carl Spaatz.

In January 1943 the 4th Fighter Group began conversion to P-47C Thunderbolts but it was not until 4 March that the first mission was flown. The Group's Thunderbolts flew interdiction strikes against airfields ahead of the bombers. 40-year old Colonel E. W. Edward Anderson the CO was given the task of bringing the 4th Fighter Group into line with USAAF procedures but his task proved difficult. His pilots were reluctant to change the lessons learned in the RAF and most pilots were unhappy about converting from the Spitfire to the Thunderbolt.

First Lieutenant John T. Godfrey and 'Reggie's Reply'. Godfrey scored a total of 16.333 victories which included 2½ Bf 109 kills flying P-47D Thunderbolts in December 1943. On 22 December flying P-47D-1-RA 42-7884 'Reggie's Reply' he was credited with the destruction of a Bf 109 and a half share in another. He was flying this aircraft on 29 November when he was awarded a Bf 109 'probable'. Godfrey was taken prisoner on 24 August 1944 when his P-51D was downed by flak. (USAF)

During the afternoon of 8 April twenty-four P-47s including some from the 4th Fighter Group took part in a 'Rodeo' set up by the RAF. The combat-experienced Lieutenant Colonel Chesley G. Peterson, 4th Fighter Group Executive and Operations Officer, led the combined force that took off from Debden and climbed to 30,000ft and then swept over Dunkirk at full power. They penetrated 12 miles into enemy territory and returned after 90 minutes without seeing any enemy fighters. On the evening of 15 April sixty P-47s including twelve in the 4th Fighter Group made another sweep of the Pas de Calais. When RAF Debden sector radioed a warning of enemy aircraft to the west of them and a swarm of fighters suddenly appeared from that direction, the P-47 pilots thought they were in for a fight only quickly to discover it was another Thunderbolt group. The 4th Fighter Group did get into a fight on this occasion when they tussled

Captain Howard D. 'Deacon' Hively of the 334th Fighter Squadron who scored twelve victories during August 1943–December 1944. (USAF)

with fifteen Fw 190A-4s of II./JG 1 over Ostend. Three Fw 190s were claimed destroyed and Major Don Blakeslee was credited with the first enemy aircraft shot down by a P-47. In fact the German unit suffered no loss. Lieutenant Colonel Chesley Peterson had to bale out into the Channel due to engine failure. He was picked up by ASR. Two 334th Fighter Squadron P-47s

Major Pierce W. McKennon in the 335th Fighter Squadron. On 20 February 1944 at the start of 'Big Week' Captain Henry L. Mills, Duane Beeson and Lieutenant Pierce W. McKennon claimed an Fw 190 apiece. On 28 august 1944 McKennon was shot down by flak near Strasbourg and he evaded until 22 September. He returned to combat status but was shot down by flak again on 18 March 1945 at Neubrandenburg air depot. He was rescued by Lieutenant George Green flying another Mustang who landed and picked him up. McKennon was killed in a flying accident near San Antonio, Texas on 18 June 1947 while flying an AT-6D. (USAF)

and their pilots fell victim to *Oberfeldwebel* Ernst Heesen of 5./ JG 1, his twenty-sixth and twenty-seventh victories.

On 4 May VIII Bomber Command dispatched seventy-nine B-17s on a five-hour round trip to the Ford and General Motors plants at Antwerp. They were escorted by twelve Allied fighter squadrons, including for the first time by six squadrons of P-47 Thunderbolts of the 4th and 56th Fighter Groups who provided fighter escort up to 175 miles. On 18 May another high-altitude

Captain (later Major) Don Gentile and his wife. Gentile scored 21.8333 victories in WWII, 16½ of them while flying the Mustang. He was killed in a flying accident (KIFA) on 28 January 1951 at Forestville, Maryland while flying a T-33A. (USAF)

'Rodeo' by the three American P-47 groups was flown along the Dutch coast. Major Don Blakeslee led his P-47s to Walcheren-Bruges-Nieuport and three P-47s bounced four Fw 190s 5,000ft below but the fighters got away. Minutes later a dozen Bf 109s approached at 30,000ft after the P-47s had turned for England at Ostend. The 109s came in astern and the P-47s broke around and dived on them. The 109s dived away in accordance with standard procedure but this was a suicidal move and the Thunderbolts turned into them with a vengeance. First Lieutenant Duane W. Beeson chased *Oberfeldwebel* Heinz Wefes of 4/JG 54 until the German baled out at 100ft for the first of the American's seventeen victories of the war. Wefes' parachute failed to open and he was killed. Second Lieutenant Robert A. Boock in the 334th Fighter Squadron was shot down and KIA by *Leutnant* Melchior Kestel of the 9th *Staffel* JG 26 in the North Sea off the coast between Knocke and Blankenberghe.

Major James A. 'Goody' Goodson of the 336th Fighter Squadron who scored fourteen confirmed victories in WWII including nine flying P-51B/D aircraft 16 March–25 May 1944. He was shot down by flak flying P-51D 44-13303 on 20 June 1944 and was taken prisoner. (USAF)

Colonel Don Blakeslee CO of the 4th Fighter Group 1 January–19 November 1944. During December 1943 he was assigned to the 354th Fighter Group to help them enter combat and he was so impressed with the Mustangs that they flew that when he returned to the 4th Fighter Group he argued forcefully to be equipped with the Mustang, which they were at the end of February 1944. Blakeslee's total victory score was 14.5, seven of which, were scored flying P-51B/D aircraft. (USAF)

On 26 June P-47s in the 4th Fighter Group led by Major Don Blakeslee on a 'Ramrod' to Gisors from Thorney Island were half way across the Channel when Blakeslee was informed that the withdrawing bombers were early. After a gradual port turn on the rendezvous point the 4th Fighter Group spotted the

Pilots in the 4th Fighter Group at Debden at briefing. (USAF)

bombers north-west of Le Tréport with enemy aircraft diving away. As the P-47s arrived six Bf 109Gs of Priller's 13th *Staffel* dived under the 334th Squadron and a combat developed 10 miles off Dieppe. Two 334th Fighter Squadron pilots, Lieutenant Raymond C. Care and Lieutenant Duane W. Beeson each claimed a Bf 109 over the Channel.

During 'Blitz Week' on 28 July P-47C Thunderbolts in the 4th Fighter Group led by Major Halsey ventured into Germany for the first time on a mission thanks to new 200-gallon unpressurized belly-tanks or 'Babies' as they came to be called. At Debden and Duxford a large number of big crates arrived yielding the new 200-gallon unpressurized auxiliary gas tanks, which were being introduced by 8th Fighter Command. The P-47C/Ds were rapidly modified to accept the tanks, which

P-51B 43-24853 VF-U in the 336th Fighter Squadron in a stream with a bent prop after a mishap. (USAF)

would permit a round trip range 30 miles deeper into enemy airspace than the 8th's fighters had previously gone. The 4th Fighter Group was tasked to provide withdrawal support for the 1st Bomb Wing to Emmerich. In spite of the new tanks being only half filled due to technical problems, the 4th Fighter Group caught the *Luftwaffe* by surprise. As the Debden Eagles arrived over Emmerich they found no bombers but passing Leerdam they spotted a different gaggle of Forts under attack by 45 to 60 enemy fighters. The 335th Squadron passed over and in front of the B-17s while the 336th Squadron went left and the 335th went to starboard to get at them. In a roaring dogfight from Germany back into Holland the 4th Fighter Group claimed three 109s and six Fw 190s. Nearing the end of the combat Lieutenant Henry I. Ayers Jnr in the 336th Fighter Squadron was shot down west of Rotterdam by *Hauptmann* Rolf Hermichen of I./JG 26. Other 'Jug' (Juggernaut–P-47 nickname) pilots heard his mayday call before he baled out to become a PoW.

On 30 July Major Halsey led the 4th Fighter Group's second belly tank mission, a 'Ramrod' withdrawal support for B-17s

Second Lieutenant Ralph 'Kid' Hofer in the cockpit of P-51B-15-NA 42-106924 QP-L 'Salem Representative'. He scored fifteen victories, all except two of them on the P-51. He was KIA on 2 July 1944 while supporting 15th AF bombers over the Balkans during an 8th AF Shuttle mission, flying P-51B 43-6746 in aerial combat at Mostar, Yugoslavia. His executioner was probably a pilot of JG 52. Probably the most colourful of all the aces, Hofer is the only one known to have been killed in combat with the Luftwaffe. *(USAF)*

to Emmerich. As the Group passed Grosbeak two groups of bombers were spotted to the north. Halsey dispatched the 335th Fighter Squadron to cover them. Some 150 to 200 enemy aircraft attacked as the squadron pulled in. The 335th Fighter Squadron claimed five Fw 190s, losing one pilot as the fight ranged over the Netherlands. After the combat, the squadron remained with the bombers until the Dutch coast. The other two squadrons continued on to the Rhine, rendezvousing with more Fortresses, flying at 27,000ft. They left the Big Friends at the coast. The 4th Fighter Group claimed a Box Score of five destroyed for one P-47 lost.

On 20 December during its withdrawal support to Münster, the 4th Fighter Group found some rich pickings. Lieutenant Colonel Don Blakeslee was leading the group and rendezvous was made with the B-17s at 26,000ft and 15 miles west of the target area. In the Enschede area of Holland four Bf 109G-5/6s of JG 26 were seen at 10/15,000ft. First Lieutenant John T. Godfrey bounced two of the fighters and Lieutenant Vasseure H. Wynn joined him in the dive. A violent dogfight ensued in which Godfrey's P-47 was severely damaged but the two Thunderbolt pilots and a third claimed three 109s destroyed. Their spirited action resulted in the deaths of *Unteroffizier* Günter Broda, *Unteroffizier* Anton Jenner and *Fähnenjunker-Feldwebel* Julius Richter.

On 7 January 1944 Lieutenant Colonel Don Blakeslee led the 4th Fighter Group in a Withdrawal Support to Ludwigshafen. Near Hesdin a dozen Fw 190s came down from above and up-sun in finger-fours to attack straggling B-17s in the lowest box. Blakeslee led the bounce, engaging the 190s in combat from 24,000 to 3,000ft. With three Focke Wulfs on his tail pumping his Thunderbolt full of holes, Blakeslee claimed one shot down. Captain James A. Goodson and Captain Robert H. Wehrman came to the rescue and Goodson downed two of the 190s. *Unteroffizier* Gerhard Guttmann of JG 26 received credit for destroying Blakeslee's Thunderbolt but that evening seventy-one holes were counted in WD-C after a forced landing at Manston.

In the afternoon of 14 January Lieutenant Colonel Selden R. Edner, the Operations Officer led the Debden Thunderbolts on a 'Freelance' to Magny-Soissons. Fifteen Fw 190s were spotted 3,000ft below and the 336th Fighter Squadron made the bounce, engaging the *Luftwaffe* from 18,000ft to the deck. Captain Don Gentile made a head-on run with two of them. They broke and he chased and shot them both down, making him an ace. With two 190s still on his tail, he heard numerous strikes all over his Thunderbolt. He turned into them and promptly ran out of ammunition, watching one of the Focke Wulfs stick to him, flown by an experienced pilot. Fifty feet over the forest of Compiègne Gentile shouted over the R/T, "Help! Help! I'm being clobbered!" Other 4th Fighter Group pilots radioed back

P-51Ds in the 335th Fighter Squadron, in September 1944. Nearest aircraft is WD-C 44-13779. (USAF)

but Gentile was too rattled to answer. All he could do was keep turning into the expert in the other cockpit. After 15 minutes of reversing turns and head-on attacks, the German pilot ran out of ammunition and both fighters turned for home. The Group re-formed and was vectored near Soissons where twelve 190s were seen 2,000ft below. The 334th Fighter Squadron made the attack, fighting all the way down to 2,000ft. Near Cambrai another four Fw 190s attacked Lieutenant Edmund D. 'Gooney Bird' Whalen and Lieutenant Alexander Rafalovich but they shared in the destruction of one of the attackers. Having claimed eight enemy aircraft destroyed for no loss, the 4th Fighter Group headed for home at 25,000ft.

On 20 February Captain James A. 'Goody' Goodson led a Withdrawal Support to Kirkburg, Germany. Five Bf 109s attacked with rockets and the 335th Fighter Squadron engaged them. Near Malmedy eight Fw 190A-6s tried to attack the first combat box of B-17s from the rear but the P-47s jumped them and they had to break off. *Unteroffizier* Erwin Hell of the 6th *Staffel* was hit and he baled out with minor injuries. Three more Fw 190s were damaged. Captain Henry L. 'Hank' Mills, Duane Beeson and Lieutenant Pierce W. McKennon claimed an Fw 190 apiece. First Lieutenant Richard I. Reed shared a Bf 110 with Lieutenant Paul S. Riley before Reed was shot down and killed NE of Koblenz by *Leutnant* Friedrich Lange of JG 26 who 20 minutes earlier had shot down B-17 'Skunkface' in the 91st Bomb Group formation.

On 24 February the 4th Fighter Group provided a Withdrawal Support north of Koblenz for Fortresses and Liberators at

P-51 44-14276 VF-A 'Martha Jane' in the 336th Fighter Squadron. (USAF)

25,000ft. As the P-47s pulled in, four Fw 190s attacked the B-24s from head-on. The 4th Fighter Group's upper squadron drove them off when four more 190s and four 109s were engaged by the other two squadrons. One Focke Wulf was claimed shot down but Lieutenant Joseph W. Sullivan was killed NW of Koblenz. On 25 February the 4th Fighter Group led by the Executive Officer, Lieutenant Colonel Selden R. Edner were flying a Penetration Support to Sedan-Stuttgart. As the P-47s rendezvoused with the B-17s near Sedan they attacked and then bounced some of the Focke Wulfs. First Lieutenant Vermont Garrison was the first to shoot down one of the enemy fighters for his 6th victory. Garrison was shot down on 3 March 1944 by flak near Boulogne flying a P-51B. His total score stood at seven victories. Flying F-86F Sabres in Korea in 1952–53 he added a further ten and two probables to his wartime score. Captain Don Gentile and Lieutenant Glenn A. Herter got two more, which also took Gentile's score to six. Then four more Fw 190s were bounced and Captain Duane Beeson and Lieutenant Pierce W. McKennon got another two to take their scores to twelve and three respectively.

P-51 44-14923 'See Me Later', 335th Fighter Squadron flown by 2nd Lieutenant Kenneth Green, one of eight Mustangs lost from a force of 743 dispatched on 3 March 1945, 'See Me Later' was hit by flak and crashed near Rotterdam. Green was taken prisoner. (Ab A. Jansen via Theo Boiten)

There was great competition among American fighter pilots to get their hands on the Mustang and Lieutenant Colonel Don Blakeslee pleaded with command to exchange their old Thunderbolts for them. But a great daylight offensive was planned, the Normandy invasion would take place within three months and so the answer was that they did not see how Blakeslee's group could become non-operational for several weeks while they retrained on to the new fighter. "That's OK, General, sir," replied Blakeslee. "We can learn to fly them on the way to the target!"

Conversion to the P-51 Mustang took place after a P-51B trainer arrived at Debden, or the 'Eagle's Nest' as it was known, on 22 February and each pilot logged about forty minutes on the new type. Command of the 4th Fighter Group passed to Don Blakeslee on 1 January. On 11 April 1944 Debden was visited by General Eisenhower who presented Distinguished Service Crosses to Lieutenant Colonel Blakeslee, Captain Don Gentile and 2nd Lieutenant Robert Johnson. 'Ike' also took a flight in the modified P-38J 'Droop Snoot' version of the Lightning.

On 8 April the 4th Fighter Group were one of the fighter groups that supported the Brunswick force. They attacked three separate gaggles of Fw 190s and Bf 109s over a 30-mile area from 23,000ft to the deck. While leading the Group near Celle Major George Carpenter claimed two Fw 190s destroyed. Altogether the Group claimed thirty-three destroyed and nine damaged. Two P-51s collided in the air west of Wittengen and 2nd Lieutenant Robert P. Claus and Captain Frank Boyles were KIA. Two other P-51 pilots were shot down and taken prisoner. Seven pilots in the 334th Squadron claimed seven fighters and a Ju 52 destroyed. They also damaged seven Bf 109s and Fw 190s and one Ju 52. The 336th Squadron destroyed thirteen and the 335 Squadron destroyed twelve.

On 24 May the Mustangs led by Major 'Goody' Goodson were among those who flew a Penetration Support on the mission to Berlin. The Mustangs climbed to 30,000ft and saw thirty–forty enemy aircraft at 35,000ft, which headed for them at 12 o'clock and a fierce air battle ensued. A red-nosed P-51 was seen to overshoot a Bf 109 at 32,000ft, which then raked

Rearming a P-51B Mustang in the 336th Fighter Squadron. (USAF)

the P-51 with cannon fire and the Mustang was last seen going down in smoke. Second Lieutenant Ralph K. Hofer, who had by now reached double figures, knocked down two more enemy fighters to take his score to twelve. Captains 'Deacon' Hively and Willard Millikan and Lieutenants Gillette, Lang, Fraser, Jones, Russel and Speer combined to claim eight other e/a destroyed. On 28 May Ralph Hofer scored his 15th and final victory when he downed a Bf 109 in the Magdeburg area. He was KIA on 2 July 1944 while supporting 15th Air Force bombers over the Balkans during an 8th Air Force Shuttle mission. Probably the most colourful of all the aces, Hofer is the only one known to have been killed in combat with the *Luftwaffe*.

On 17 September during 'Market Garden' for four pilots killed in action JG 26 claimed five Mustangs including two in the 4th Fighter Group P-51s. The Group was being led by the CO Lieutenant Colonel Kinnard on Area Patrol from Harderwijk, Netherlands to Wesel, Germany when fifteen Focke Wulfs bounced a few P-51s in the 335th Squadron. Although the 4th Fighter Group was credited with six Fw 190s only two were lost.

On 5 December 1944 Major Howard 'Deacon' Hively CO, 334th Fighter Squadron shot down an Fw 190A-8 north-west of Nordhorn while the Group was escorting two 'Aphrodite' B-17s (packed with the explosive torpex and flown over the North Sea when the pilot and co-pilot baled out and the drone B17 was directed to its target in Europe by a Ventura 'mother ship'.) Hively's victim – his twelfth and final victory of the war – was *Oberfeldwebel* Friedrich Buscheggar of 2./JG 26 who was killed when he attempted to land his badly shot up fighter at Marburg north-west of Furstenau.

The 4th Fighter Group's combined claims of 583¼ air victories and 469 enemy aircraft destroyed on the ground was the largest for any unit of the USAAF. The Group also received a Distinguished Unit Citation for operations between 5 March and 24 April 1944 in which 189 air and 134 ground victories were claimed. The 4th Fighter Group flew its last mission on 25 April 1945. In two years and seven months 241 of its fighters were missing in action. The Group remained at Debden, until July 1945 and the last Americans left on 5 September and Debden reverted to RAF control. Debden's control tower was demolished in 1971. The station officially closed on 21 August 1975.

Duxford (Station 357)

This world-famous airfield, which dates from the First World War when RAF Duxford opened officially in September 1918, was one of the most important RAF Fighter Command front line stations in 1940 during the Battle of Britain period. Prior to the United States' entry into WWII 244 Americans pilots flew in the Eagle Squadrons of RAF Fighter Command. On 1 August 1941 No. 133 'Eagle' Squadron was established at Coltishall and during the following weeks it was moved to three other stations, Duxford, Colly Weston and then Fowlmere. This squadron was one of three American units – 71, 121 and 133 Squadron – that were formed late in 1940. To equip 133 Squadron, motto 'Let us to the battle', eighteen Hurricane IIB fighters armed with four 20mm cannon were flown in. Early in October 1941 133 fled the Eagle's Nest at Duxford and moved to Fowlmere.

P-47 Thunderbolt 'Leaky Joe' at Bassingbourn. At the end of 1942 the P-47 was the only readily available American produced high-performance fighter. 200 were sent to Britain in December 1942 and January 1943. (USAF)

Major Eugene Roberts CO of the 84th Fighter Squadron. On 28 July 1943, during 'Blitz Week', the 56th and 78th Fighter Groups carried unpressurized 200-gal ferry tanks below the centre fuselage for the first time. On 30 July, when they escorted the Fortresses almost to Kassel and back again, flying 'Spokane Chief', Roberts scored the first 'hat trick' of 'kills' (two Fw 190s and an Bf 109), thus becoming the first US pilot to notch a triple victory in Europe. (via Andy Height)

On 12 August 1942 1st Lieutenant J. A. Glenn of the 1st Fighter Group, USAAC, became the first American pilot to arrive at Duxford when he flew a Lockheed P-38F Lightning in from Goxhill on tactical trials. In October a nucleus of officers of the 350th Fighter Group arrived at Duxford. This Group had the use of a number of Spitfires and P-39 Airacobras for working-up purposes, but the late arrival of ground crews from the USA slowed this process down. By January 1943 the Group was at full strength and soon began the journey to North Africa.

In December 1942 homesick Americans in the 78th Fighter Group at Goxhill, a remote airfield in the flat Lincolnshire Fenland were hopelessly looking forward to a cold, and wet and cheerless first Christmas in the ETO. At the start of the New Year the 78th had to begin exchanging their Lightnings for P-47C Thunderbolts. After losing their P-38s only fifteen of the

Major Eugene P. Roberts, CO of the 84th Fighter Squadron, indicating the two kills that made him an ace on 24 August 1943 when he shot down a Bf 109 and an Fw 190. Roberts commanded the 84th Fighter Squadron August 1942–28 September 1943 and was then deputy CO of the Group until 17 December 1943. He flew eighty-nine combat missions with the 78th Fighter Group, during which time he scored nine victories and one probable, all in P-47Cs. All except two of his victories were achieved flying P-47C-5R-RE 41-6330 'Spokane Chief'. Lieutenant Colonel Roberts transferred to 8th FC and flew a second tour as commander of the 364th Fighter Group, which was equipped with P-51D Mustangs, 3 January–November 1945. (USAF)

original pilots remained and these included Colonel Peterson, his deputies, the three squadron commanders, operations officers and flight leaders. The situation was a massive blow

P-47C-5R-RE 41-6330 'Spokane Chief'. (USAF)

especially since the air echelon considered the Thunderbolt a poor substitute for the Lightning although the maintenance was appreciably easier than with the P-38. In the spring Goxhill's reluctant American inhabitants received a boost with the news that they were heading south, to Station 357 Duxford, nearer to civilization with Cambridge the local watering hole. Apparently, Duxford was a permanent pre-war RAF station, which was rumoured to have all the attributes of a 'country-club' atmosphere. Any change from the mud and basic living accommodation at Goxhill just had to be good, especially as the Group had been destined for a 'temporary' base at Halesworth in rural Suffolk.

On 18 March orders were given for all RAF units to leave Duxford and on 24 March a convoy of vehicles arrived at the main gate carrying the US advance party. The Group, including HO staff, comprised 1,700 men. Almost to a man they were very pleased with the quality of the accommodation. Imposing red brick buildings, some of them camouflaged, standard for the RAF, mottled with ubiquitous tans, greens and greys, were everything they had been led to believe. The hangars, too, were

The 84th Fighter Squadron at Duxford, June 1943. Major Eugene Roberts, the CO, is second from right, front row. The 78th Fighter Group was based at the famous Battle of Britain station from 3 April 1943, having previously been based at Goxhill and after first flying the P-38, changed to the P-47C in January 1943. (via Andy Height)

conveniently located and the only signs of mud were those left by spring rain showers on the large grass airfield. Two-storey brick barracks that housed non-commissioned officers and enlisted men were still more comfortable than the corrugated metal Quonset huts occupied by their counterparts at other fighter and bomber group bases. The Control Tower was typical of those on RAF airfields, a squat two-story building that resembled one box stacked on another. There was a wide expanse of windows in front and on the sides and an upper viewing deck, or veranda, with a handrail round it. Controllers directed local aircraft traffic from the upper storey, and dignitaries who later visited the base often reviewed take-off and landings from the viewing deck. Soon, wooden huts would spring up and more buildings and some blister hangars began to appear. Squadron dispersal could be cold and wet, the hours were long, and the men were going to be as comfortable as they could! Many of the brick barracks were fitted with modern casement windows and they were centrally heated. All of them had electric lights and some had tiled shower rooms. The buildings on the airfield

Flight Officer (later 1st Lieutenant) Pete E. Pompetti in the cockpit of P-47C-5-RE 41-6393 WZ-R 'Darkie' in the 84th Fighter Squadron at Duxford with his ground crew. Pompetti scored his first victory, a Bf 109, in this aircraft on 30 July 1943. He had been credited with five confirmed victories on P-47C/Ds when on 17 March 1944 he was downed by flak and taken prisoner on his 95th combat mission. (via Andy Height)

and the living site opposite were beautifully landscaped with trees, flowers and shrubs. Lawns were kept close cropped and the flower beds were well tended, partially because of their beauty, but also to aid aerial camouflage, making the entire airfield appear to be another sleepy but picturesque English village. The roads were paved and there were paths to walk on. Many of the buildings were covered with ivy while hedges hid the barbed wire. There were garages and four large hangars to accommodate mobile and air equipment. The two-storeyed mess hall building had four dining bays and two steam tables kept food hot for serving. The kitchen was one of the few in the ETO with steam cooking apparatus. From the start china plates were issued but enlisted personnel had to bring their own utensils and cups. The dispensary housed dental clinics, doctors' examination rooms and offices, a first aid room, and treatment rooms. Thriplow House, a large mansion two miles away was converted into sick quarters and rest area for station personnel. Motor ambulances took serious injuries and hospital cases to general hospitals nearby.

First Lieutenant (later Captain) Huie Lamb in front of his P-47 at Duxford. The distinctive black-and-white chequerboard squares applied to the engine cowling shutters were introduced during the first week of April 1944. (via Andy Height)

Having moved in, the Group quickly settled down and began working up the three squadrons, the 82nd, 83rd and 84th Fighter Squadrons, to operational status. During the week 1 to 6 April 75 P-47C Thunderbolt aircraft were finally flown in. On 15 June 1943, Duxford was officially handed over to the Eighth Air Force. The 78th Fighter Group remained at Duxford until the end of hostilities, flying 450 missions. The majority of those flown in 1943 were on bomber escort.

On 4 May VIII Bomber Command dispatched seventy-nine B-17s on a five-hour round trip to the Ford and General Motors plants at Antwerp. They were escorted by twelve Allied fighter squadrons, including for the first time by six squadrons of P-47 Thunderbolts of the 4th and 56th Fighter Groups who provided fighter escort up to 175 miles. More than thirty B-17s and B-24s that flew diversionary feints towards the French coast succeeded in drawing over 100 German fighters away from the main force and they returned without loss after sixty-five bombers had got their bombs away on the factory. In four

P-51D Mustangs of the 84th Fighter Squadron in one of the First World War hangars at Duxford. Nearest aircraft is P-51D 44-63779 WZ-G flown by 1st Lieutenant Alfred A. Garback. The 'GAUNTLET ENDURANCE AT NORMAL CRUISING SPEED' lettering refers to the 1930s when Gloster Gauntlets of 19 Squadron were stationed there, the biplane fighters having an endurance of two hours, which was in contrast to the Mustangs and their 7–8 hour endurance. The 78th Fighter Group, like their RAF 19 Squadron predecessors, whose Gauntlets were adorned with light blue and white chequers on wings and fuselage, adopted equally bold markings using a black and white chequerboard scheme. (via Ian McLachlan)

hours 8th Bomber Command had attacked four targets, losing twelve B-17s and B-24s and claiming sixty-seven fighters shot down. RAF Spitfires and USAAF Thunderbolts had given excellent fighter cover on the Antwerp and Courtrai raids. The 78th Fighter Group, with three squadrons of sixteen P-47s each led by Colonel Arman Peterson encountered more than twenty Focke-Wulf l90s and Me 109s at 20,000–24,000ft in the Antwerp area and dogfights broke out all over the sky. Major James J. Stone, CO of the 83rd Squadron, claimed an Fw 190, which was heading for the bombers. Captain Robert E. Adamina also claimed an Fw 190 while Captain Jack J. Oberhansly and Captain Charles P. London got 'probables.' Colonel Peterson and four other pilots each damaged a 190. Adamina, Captain

Removing engine panels from a 78th Fighter Group Thunderbolt. (USAF)

Elmer E. McTaggart and Flight Officer S. R. Martinek were shot down. Martinek was taken prisoner. McTaggart lost 25lb in weight while evading capture. He worked his way southward across the Pyrenees into Spain. Adamina rode his T-bolt down to the water and ditched successfully.

On 16 May a fighter sweep by eleven P-47s of the 4th, 56th and 78th Fighter Groups was flown over northern Belgium. This resulted in combat action when they met thirty fighters of JG 1 in the Vlissingen area being led by the *Geschwader Kommodore*, Major Hans 'Fips' Philipp, an ex-JG54 *Experte*, who had assumed command of JG 1 on 1 April. Philipp claimed a P-47 as his 205th *Abschuss*, followed one minute later by another 'Jug' shot down by *Oberleutnant* Koch as his 16th kill. Colonel Arman Peterson, 78th Fighter Group CO, destroyed one Fw 190 and two more fell to the guns of his Group. There was only one victim, *Hauptmann* Dietrich Wickop, *Kommandeur,* II./JG 1 who had thirteen victories, including three B-17s.

On 22 June 1943 during the first really deep penetration mission to Hüls, *Hauptmann* 'Wutz' Galland and the IInd *Gruppe* JG26 reached the Fortresses as they were leaving the target and they attacked from the rear. They made repeated attacks and were out of ammunition when the P-47s of the 4th and 78th

P-47D-28-RE 44-19566 with D-Day markings at Duxford. (via Andy Height)

Fighter Groups finally arrived to provide withdrawal support. The Thunderbolts claimed seven Fw 190s and a Bf 109 for no loss.

On 14 July 1943, Fw 190s of I/JG 2 and Bf 109s of II/JG 2 took on the 4th Fighter Group P-47s to the west of the Somme near Le Treport. Major 'Wutz' Galland and his pilots battled with the P-47s of the 78th Fighter Group near Hesdin. Major Harry Dayhuff had led his group to Hornoy, where they had made rendezvous with B-17s bombing Amiens. Near Montreiul, as he led the 82nd and the 84th Squadrons into a large group of Fw 190s heading for the bombers at Lelouget, more enemy aircraft joined the fight. First Lieutenant Donald Jackson was killed when he was struck by gunfire from the B-17s in the chase.

In the ensuing air battle 'Wutz' Galland claimed a 78th Fighter Group P-47 over the north bank of the Somme Estuary north-west of Hesdin and he claimed another 10–15 km west of Etaples. Second Lieutenant August V. DeGenaro in the 82nd Squadron flew the first of these P-47s. He had the right side of his canopy and instrument panel shot out causing shell splinter wounds in his hands, ankles and right knee. At first he thought he was going to die but he quickly recovered and got 'damned mad', diving to 2,000ft into a swarm of FWs where he shot one down from 100 yards, probably destroyed another and

P-47 42-25871 'Nigger II' flown by Captain Richard M. Holly CO, 84th Fighter Squadron. The Thunderbolt was named after Holly's always-suntanned wife. This same photo is displayed behind the bar at the Red Lion in Whittlesford. (via Andy Height)

damaged a third. Then he headed for the Channel, ducking into low clouds to evade three more FWs that followed him almost to the coast. All this time DeGenaro was flying his plane with no instruments and controlling it with his forearms only. The right aileron was gone and the right wing and tail were badly damaged. A crash landing was out of the question because he had unhooked his safety belt in combat and he could not re-hook it. DeGenero recalled:

I headed out to sea again to bale out because I was afraid that if I baled out over land the plane would crash into one of the towns along the coast. I knew I was over England, because I saw the cliffs of Dover. I saw a fishing boat just off shore and decided to bale out near it. The canopy of my plane had jammed and would not open, but since some of the glass had been shot away, I was able to punch and force my way through the canopy, bale out and open my chute. The fishing boat picked me up at once. If it had not, I would have drowned,

Lieutenant William S. Swanson of the 82nd Fighter Squadron, in the cockpit of his P-47D-6-RE 42-74733. Swanson was KIA on 11 February 1944. (USAF)

because I was unable to undo my parachute harness and was getting weak from loss of blood.

Later in hospital DeGenero was awarded the DSC for valour and sent home to recover from his wounds Major 'Wutz' Galland's second P-47 that he claimed also made it back to England where the pilot baled out into the Channel and he was rescued.

On 30 July 1943, as the 78th Fighter Group pilots went into briefing they knew it was going to be an unusual mission. The

P-47Cs of the 82nd Fighter Squadron at Bassingbourn in late 1944. Nearest aircraft is P-47D-27-RE 42-27339 with two 108-gallon tanks and a 150-gallon belly tank. Below the cockpit are eight victory swastikas denoting kills by Major (later Brig Gen) Joe E. Myers who was credited with three victories flying the P-38 and 1½ victories flying this P-47D including his last on 7 October 1944 when he destroyed a Bf 109 in the Leipzig area. Behind is P-47D-22-RE 42-26387 'Miss Behave'. (USAF)

ground crews realized that recently arrived drop tanks denoted a long haul and the big briefing map confirmed it. It was to be withdrawal support for 186 B-17s in the 1st and 4th Wings going to Kassel, a round trip of 600 miles, when Bomber Command brought down the curtain on 'Blitz Week' with take-off at 0854 hours. The weather was fine and the new tanks meant that the P-47s could escort the heavies almost to the target and back again. Without the P-47s losses would have been on an alarming scale because the Fortress formations were hit by a ferocious onslaught of enemy fighters. As the 78th Fighter Group approached the enemy coast, the new belly tanks were dropped 15 miles offshore of the Hook of Holland. The P-47s then climbed to penetration altitude as they flew on over Rotterdam and Nijmegen and entered Germany near Kleve before heading for the Rendezvous Point at Haltern. Nearing the rendezvous, the bombers were sighted at 11 o'clock 20 miles north and the 78th turned left at 28,000ft, 4,000ft above their charges and began to take up station. Shortly after the turn, the 78th lost its second Group commander in less than a month (Colonel Arman Peterson having being KIA on 1 July) when Lieutenant Colonel Melvin F. McNickle's oxygen system failed and he lost consciousness. McNickle collided with his wingman, 1st Lieutenant James Byers, near Winterswijk, Netherlands. Byers baled out but he also died. When McNickle regained consciousness, he was still strapped in his cockpit in the wreckage of his inverted crashed P-47 with the Dutch Underground trying to extricate him. McNickle had two broken shoulders and other serious wounds. The intervention by just over 100 P-47s in the 4th, 56th and 78th Fighter Groups prevented further bomber losses. They claimed twenty-four enemy fighters shot down, the 78th Fighter Group claiming seven Bf 109s and nine Fw 190s, including three, the first triple victory in the ETO, by Major Eugene P. Roberts in the 84th Fighter Squadron, who was flying '*Spokane Chief*'. For fighting off superior numbers of enemy fighters in getting his triple, Major Eugene P. Roberts won the group's second Distinguished Service Cross within a month.

On 1 November 1943 Colonel Fred Gray, the CO, called the entire Group to the base theatre and announced that they were being re-equipped with the P-51D Mustang. Captain Pete Keillor recalls:

We were told that we would be changing from the good old P-47s that would stand almost any punishment to P-51s, which were an unknown quantity, and no one wanted to change. One story on the P-47 concerned a pilot in the 84th before the invasion. He was strafing in France when he ran into a cable. It cut off the bottom four cylinders of the front row on his engine and he made it back across the Channel and crash landed in England. Try that with any other plane. One of our planes that I saw came back with a hole a couple of feet in diameter right at the left wing root. The pilot could have got out of the cockpit and jumped through the hole.

As if coming to terms with all the aircraft changes was not enough, prolonged winter rains had turned Duxford airfield, (which appropriately was nicknamed 'The Duckpond') into a mud patch completely unsuitable for fighter operations. On

Captain Ben I. Mayo of the 82nd Fighter Squadron in the cockpit of P-47D 'No Guts – No Glory!' Mayo is credited with the destruction of four enemy aircraft while flying P-47s as CO of both the 84th and 82nd Fighter Squadron during June to September 1944. His first victory was a Bf 109 on D+1 and his second victory, another Bf 109, followed on 20 June. (USAF)

17 November the aircraft and many personnel were moved to Bassingbourn airfield 14 miles west. The move was made to allow US Army Engineers to put down a 3,500 ft long by 150 ft wide Pierced Steel Planking (PSP) main runway in between two steel mattings laid down at each end of the field in 1943. (This had helped while the aircraft were stationary but trying to take off or land in water was no joke). When added to the mats at either end the total length would be 4,100 ft. Work was held up for a time because the majority of PSP matting had been sent to France for the construction of advanced airfields there and in any case everyone thought that it was no longer needed in England. Bassingbourn was a pre-war airfield built for the RAF and the B-17s of the 91st Bomb Group had a tarmac runway for landing and taking off but the dispersal areas were just as muddy as Duxford's. They became badly congested with

bombers and fighters when they flew missions from the same airfield, although there were no delays during the fighters' sojourn at the bomber base. Before each mission take-off the ground crews and armourers who still lived at Duxford had to be brought over in trucks. It was very cold on the remote dispersals at Bassingbourn and permanent accommodation was at premium. Each fighter squadron's engineering and supply section was housed in a single pyramid tent on the airfield with a direct telephone line to Duxford so parts could be sent for quickly.

The first mission from Bassingbourn was flown on 21 November when the Group was part of the escort for 366 B-24s attacking oil refineries at Hamburg. On Friday 26 November 633 bombers, the largest formation ever assembled by 8th Bomber Command were directed against targets as far apart as Bremen and Paris. P-47s escorted the bombers from the target. Twenty-nine B-17s and five fighters were lost. Almost all the heavies lost came from the main raid on Bremen. German claimants came from II./JG 27, IV./NJG 1 (attacking stragglers over northern Holland) and ZG 26 *Zerstören*. Eighty-six enemy fighters were claimed destroyed, twenty-six of them by B-17 gunners. At Chantilly at 1040 hours *Oberfeldwebel* Adolf 'Addi' Glunz claimed a 78th Fighter Group P-47. The Group had taken off and headed for mid-Channel where they made rendezvous with 128 B-17s of the 3rd Bomb Division. After taking up escort above the bomber stream, the force flew the route of Dieppe-Montford-Evreaux to the target, a bearing industry at Montdidier near Paris. As the Forts made their turn for the target east of Paris, about thirty German fighters went into attacks on the bomber's front and rear ranks. Major Jack Price started firing at a Fw 190 from 550 yards to prevent it making a head-on pass at the bombers. He got good strikes all over the German and closed to 100 yards before he had to break off to avoid running into the bombers. The Fw 190 stalled and went down trailing smoke. Next Price caught a climbing Bf 109, came in astern at 300 yards and exploded it in flames. Howard Askelson closed to 200 yards with an out-of-the-sun astern run at three Bf 109s near bomber level and sent one straight down in fire and lots of black smoke.

'Come and get it' at Duxford Mess. (USAF)

The battle went on in a running fight until the force reached the Beauvais area, where 1st Lieutenant Warren M. Wesson took a long 600 yard shot at the line of flight of an Fw 190 and held his trigger down as the German passed through his fire. Another pilot who saw the Fw crash confirmed the victory. Three of the Group's P-47s crash-landed in England.

On 11 December the new runway at Duxford was ready for operational missions and the Group returned home. Five days later about thirty P-51D Mustangs were flown in from the air depot and parked on the grass around the control tower. All the Mustangs of course had to be fitted out and inspected and painted in the Group markings with the nose of each P-51 having the familiar white and black chequers added to the sleek natural-metal skin.

On 24 January 1944 bad weather during assembly played havoc with assembly procedures. At Duxford Earl Payne watched the 'Big fleets' of bombers taking off for Germany. He saw a B-17 flying near the field, which happened to blow up in mid-air before crashing into the hills beyond. (B-17 42-40009 in the 324th

Bomb Squadron, 91st Bomb Group flown by Lieutenant Marco DeMara). Payne counted six parachutes and they seemed to take a long time to get down. Four landed out of sight but two landed near the roundabout out of Whittlesford. One of the chutes failed to open because it was burned. 'The poor fellow landed on his feet, which were driven clear up to his stomach and burst his lungs. His entrails coming out of either side of his body beneath his armpits.' the 78th Fighter Group carried out a diversionary patrol of the Malmedy-St. Vith, area in Belgium. South-west of Brussels the P-47s were bounced by Fw 190s who claimed two P-47s shot down though none were lost.

On 16 March a flight of P-47s in the 84th Fighter Squadron led by 1st Lieutenant Quince L. Brown spotted enemy fighters in a landing pattern. They were easy prey. Brown led his flight down to the deck. Chopping throttle and skidding to slow down, he got behind a Bf 109 and at 50 yards he fired, scoring hits. The 109 flamed and crashed to the left of the runway. Brown then saw a parked Ju 88 ahead of him and torched it with a short burst. Climbing to 7,000ft, Brown encountered two Fw 190s coming at him from 9 o'clock. *Leutnant* Klaus Kunze of 1st *Staffel* piloted one of them. As Brown got into a left-hand Lufbery Circle with the two Fw 190s, (It was a Major Lufberg who, in the First World War, devised a defensive tactic of several aircraft flying in a tight circle, thereby making it difficult for attacking aircraft to penetrate without themselves being attacked) the wingman deserted his leader, who kept trying to out climb and outturn the P-47 but Brown used water-injection and he caught up with Kunze who dived through the clouds followed by the Thunderbolt. Keeping Kunze in his sights and firing at 350 yards, Brown watched the Fw 190 roll on its back smoking and crash into a small creek. The German pilot was killed. With his wingman, Brown again climbed through the clouds and discovered two Bf 109s trying to tag them from behind. All the Messerschmitts went into a Lufbery turning battle and again the German wingman split from his leader. The leader then tried to outrun the P-47s on top of the clouds but the Thunderbolts stayed with him without resorting to water-injection. Brown cut him off from a hole in the clouds and scored hits. The leader was last seen going vertical

Major Quince Brown in the 84th Fighter Squadron, whose P-47 was hit by flak on 6 September 1944. He succeeded in baling out only to be apprehended by an SS officer who murdered him in cold blood with a pistol shot to the back of his head. Brown had scored 12.333 victories. (USAF)

into the clouds with heavy smoke streaming from his engine and wing roots. In all three Bf 109s were shot down and their pilots injured. Quince Brown was awarded the Silver Star for this four-kill mission. In April he was promoted Captain and further promotion to major followed. He went on leave to the US after his first tour, returning to the 84th Fighter Squadron on 28 August 1944. On 1 September he scored his 12th and final victory. Five days later he was shot down by flak 2km west of Schleiden. He baled out and was murdered by a *Schutzstaffel SS* officer.

On 19 July 1944 John Putnam and Martin Smith waited expectantly for the arrival of their buddy, Lieutenant James

A. Sasser, a B-17 pilot at Horham, Suffolk. Sasser had been a member of the 84th Squadron before joining the 95th Bomb Group. He appeared over the field in his B-17, *'Ready Freddie'* with three other crewmembers on board. They landed and picked up Putnam and eight other members of his Squadron. Sasser then took off and proceeded to buzz the control tower. 'Ready Freddie' headed towards the tower and the technical site from the east only a few feet above the flying field. Sasser judged his pull up over the tower accurately but evidently did not see the warning blinker light mast on top of the 84th Squadron's hangar behind the tower. *'Ready Freddie'* clipped the mast and the impact sheered off part of the left wing, which folded back and tore off the left horizontal stabilizer and part of the rudder. The B-17 rolled inverted to the left over the top of the Officers' Club, dropping the stabilizer on the lawn outside and the wing section on its roof while a fuel tank landed on an empty hut. *'Ready Freddie'* crashed into the main barrack block of the 83rd Squadron. All thirteen men on board were killed. Smith, who died in the crash, had just eight hours remaining to finish his tour. Sergeant Ernest Taylor, who was in the barracks, also died. Two others were badly burned. The Fortress was fully loaded with fuel and the barrack block burned for three hours and was destroyed. With the help of the Cambridge Fire Department, base firefighters finally managed to extinguish the flames. Captain William J. Zink the Chaplain made two unsuccessful attempts to rescue the man in the barracks. At first unable to reach him because of fumes and smoke, Zink dashed out, grabbed a gas mask and helmet and re-entered the building but falling beams and fire stopped him. Then he gave last rites for the victims and helped medical personnel extricate bodies from the wreckage of the bomber. He was presented with the Soldiers Medal for his actions and thus became the first 8th Air Force chaplain to receive the award. Flames gutted most of one Squadron building while pieces, which hit the officers' barracks and a barracks caused lesser damage. After the crash, squadrons held formations and checked rolls carefully for men missing in the accident. Had the accident occurred thirty minutes or so later, at least a hundred men would have been in the building because by then the crewmen would have been in off the line.

On 14 January 1945 the 78th Fighter Group claimed six Fw 190D-9s and half a dozen Bf 109G/Ks during a combat with II Gruppe JG 26. Among the dead and missing was *Ritterkreuzträger Oberleutnant* Gerhard Vogt CO 5th *Staffel* who had forty-eight victories. Major Anton 'Toni' Hackl returned to receive confirmation of a 78th Fighter Group P-51, his 175th victory. A second mission flown by the 78th Fighter Group later in the day ran the kill tally to 14-0-14 when the 83rd Squadron's red flight bounced 4 Fw 190s in the traffic pattern of an airfield north of Diepholz.

In all, the 78th Fighter Group destroyed 338½ enemy aircraft and 358½ on the ground. It was awarded Distinguished Unit Citations for action in support of the airborne forces in Holland in September 1944 and for ground strafing in Czechoslovakia in April 1945. It lost 167 aircraft missing in action, flying 450 missions.

On 1 December 1945 Duxford was officially returned to the RAF. For the next sixteen years, Duxford remained an RAF Fighter Command station, although it closed in October 1949 to have a single concrete runway, a new perimeter track and apron laid down. The station reopened in August 1951. On 1 August 1961, a Meteor NF.l4 made the last take-off from the runway before Duxford officially closed as an RAF airfield.

In the summer of 1968 the airfield was one of the locations for the filming of *Battle of Britain*. On 21 and 22 June one of the original WWI Belfast hangars was blown up in stages for the filming and the airfield was spectacularly filmed from the air in a realistic bombing sequence. Duxford never received any significant bomb attack during WW2 whereas North Weald did. The French chateau, seen at the beginning of the film, was constructed on the south-west corner of the airfield.

Today Duxford airfield is jointly owned by the Cambridgeshire County Council and the Imperial War Museum and is one of the premier museums in the world. The Ministry of Defence declared its intention to dispose of Duxford airfield in 1969. The Imperial War Museum had been looking for a suitable site for the storage, restoration and eventual display of exhibits too large for its headquarters in London. In 1977 Cambridgeshire County

Council, the IWM and the Duxford Aviation Society bought the runway to give the aerodrome a new lease of life. Today Duxford is established as the European Centre of aviation history. Air shows are a regular feature during the summer months, even though 1,000ft of the post-war runway extension was lost when the M11 motorway was built in 1977. In 1986 Sir Norman Foster & Partners were first approached by the Imperial War Museum and given a brief to centralise and preserve the Museum's collection of American aircraft. Construction of the American Air Museum in Britain began in September 1995.

East Wretham (Station 133)
This airfield in Breckland was brought into service when 311 (Czech) Squadron at Honington operated from the remote satellite airfield from mid September until April 1942. In November that same year 115 Squadron's Wellington III and later Lancasters, occupied the aerodrome until the USAAF took over in 1943. It was originally planned to bring the airfield up to Class A standard for bomber use but this work was not carried out. The landing area was 1,880 yards by 1,400 yards and eventually a pierced-steel planking runway was laid.

P-51Ds of the 368th Fighter Squadron in finger-four formation over Merseberg in 1944. 44-14652 'Betty Louise' CV-L is nearest the Brownie camera of Eugene F. Britton. 44-14500 Griffin is next. Rudder markings were yellow and the cowlings bright green. (E. F. Britton via Ian McLachlan)

There were two main T2 hangars. A service road ran round the boundary of the flying field and this and the twenty-eight hardstands were macadam-surfaced. The USAAF laid steel matting and four blister hangars were erected at various points around the airfield and one of steel frame with canvas covering. Nissen huts housed 190 officers and 1,519 enlisted men.

The 359th Fighter Group equipped with P-47 Thunderbolts arrived in October 1943 and became operational in December. The group converted to the Mustang in late April 1944 and these aircraft were painted with green spinners and nosebands.

On 11 September forty-nine Mustangs in the 359th Fighter Group were assigned the task of providing penetration, target and withdrawal support to bombardment forces attacking oil plants in the Merseburg area. They were to pick the B-17s up at 22,000ft in the Blankenheim area at 1030. Major Ben King and Major Bill Forehand were leaders. Rendezvous was perfect and 25 minutes later battles raged that resulted in the Group's greatest day. The score: thirty-five enemy planes destroyed; four probably destroyed and eighteen damaged. It all began in the vicinity of Gissen when thirty Bf 109s and Fw 190s were sighted at 32,000ft preparing to attack the trailing bombardment formation. The 359th Fighter Group pilots immediately dispersed and drove the hostile fighters to the deck destroying one and damaging

two. Constantly on the alert for possible interception a number of enemy aircraft were observed taking off from an airfield near Gotha at 1130 hours and they aggressively dived to attack. The Mustang pilots outmanoeuvred and destroyed five Bf 109s in the air and then in the face of anti-aircraft fire strafed and destroyed four Ju 88s and Me-

Captain (later Major) Ray S. Wetmore in the 370th Fighter Squadron, who destroyed 21.25 e/a February 1944–March 1945 flying P-47s and P-51B/D Mustangs. (USAF)

Green nosed P-51Bs and Ds of the 369th Fighter Squadron (IV) and 370th Fighter Squadron (CS) in formation. Each fighter group totalled forty-eight aircraft in three squadrons. After being relieved of escort duties, and if fuel reserves were adequate, fighter leaders were allowed to take their formations down to strafe airfields in the target area. (USAF)

210s and damaged four others. Shortly thereafter an estimated thirty Bf 109s and Fw 190s were sighted heading east at 30,000ft on the bomber track. Although outnumbered, an element of the 359th destroyed two and damaged another. At 1130 hours over 100 hostile fighters were seen at 30,000ft north of the bomber formation and the 359th pilots immediately proceeded towards the enemy. They destroyed four, probably destroyed two and damaged one and then in individual dogfights destroyed four more enemy planes. Meanwhile other pilots of the groups descended to a grass landing ground in the vicinity of Kelleda, Germany and in dividing offensive tactics destroyed four and damaged nine parked aircraft. At 1203 hours in the vicinity

Three Mustangs of the 359th Fighter Group. A new P-51D, 44-13669 'CV-I' 'Pegelin' in the 368th Squadron, which accompanies two P-51Bs from the same unit, has yet to receive its fin fillet. (via Mike Bailey)

of Eisleben after the target had been bombed fifteen Fw 190s executed vicious attacks on the bomber formation. The 359th destroyed six of the enemy aircraft, probably destroyed an additional two and damaged one other. On the return to home base the P-51s destroyed seven locomotives.

Altogether, the 359th Fighter Group flew 346 fighter missions from East Wretham, claiming 253 aircraft destroyed in the air and ninety-eight on the ground and losing 106 aircraft. The Group began returning to the USA in late October 1945. East Wretham airfield was abandoned shortly after the war and is now part of the Army's Stanford Practical Training Area. Most of the original airfield buildings, including a T2 hangar, remain.

Fowlmere (Station 378)

Fowlmere had been a grass airfield in the First World War although all the hangars were demolished after hostilities had ended. In the 1930s it was intended as a satellite for Duxford and was used in the Battle of Britain by No. 19 Squadron's Spitfires. During the winter of 1943–44 the airfield was expanded for use as a USAAF fighter airfield. Two PSP runways were laid, one of 1,600 yards running NE-SW and the other of 1,400 yards on an E–W axis. Accommodation was built to house 190 officers and 1,519 enlisted men. Soon after Duxford was transferred to the 8th Air Force in 1943, Fowlmere became an airfield in its own right

P-51D-15-NA Mustangs 'Develess 3rd' and 44-15016 'Heat Wave' in the 369th Fighter Squadron. Near Merseberg, on 21 November 1944, First Lieutenant Claude J. Crenshaw from Monroe. Louisiana, flying 'Heat Wave', shot down four Fw 190s and claimed a probable to take his wartime score to seven confirmed kills. This tally is even more impressive considering that only three of his guns were working! Crenshaw had scored his first victories on 11 September when he shot down two Bf 109s and he added a third seven days later. 'Heat Wave' was just one of three Mustangs that Crenshaw was assigned during his seven-month tour with the 369th. Crenshaw, who also scored three ground strafing kills completed his tour with 270 combat hours. (via Tony Chardella)

as Station 378 with P-51B Mustangs of the 339th Fighter Group stationed there. With the 78th and 339th Fighter Groups the 339th was part of the 66th Fighter Wing with HQ at Sawston Hall. While the PSP matting was laid at Fowlmere the 339th Fighter Group was moved temporarily to Bassingbourn. At Fowlmere a T2 hangar was erected on the small RAF technical site which had grown up around the farm buildings on the northern perimeter. Seven smaller blister hangars were situated in squadron areas around the field. Nissen hut accommodation housed 1,700 personnel in sites adjacent to the village of Fowlmere.

The 339th Fighter Group remained at Fowlmere or 'Hen Puddle', as it was known, for 12 months of operations. On 5 April 1944 the 339th Fighter Group equipped with P-51B Mustangs

P-51D 44-13808 D7-U in the 503rd Fighter Squadron. (USAF)

arrived and became operational at the end of the month. All the Mustangs were painted with red and white chequerboard nose markings.

It is not widely known that Lieutenant Bert Stiles who had flown a tour of missions as a B-17 co-pilot in the 91st Bomb Group at Bassingbourn before transferring to fighters was shot down and killed while serving with the 339th. Stiles wrote the classic *Serenade to the Big Bird,* one of the finest books in aviation literature while flying a thirty-five mission tour 19 April-20 July 1944. Stiles flew co-pilot to Sam Newton on seventeen missions up until 12 June 1944 and then flew his last five missions as co-pilot to W. R. Langford (1) and Lieutenant W. Green to complete his bomber tour. Instead of returning to America on leave now due to him, Stiles asked to be transferred to fighters and he moved to the 339th Fighter Group and to P-51s. At age 23, he was shot down and killed on 26 November 1944 while escorting bombers to Hanover.

The 339th was awarded a Distinguished Unit Citation for the destruction of fifty-eight enemy aircraft on escort missions on 10–11 September 1944. The Group's main claim to fame was having the highest claims of air and ground victories in one year.

P-51B 43-7180/M and P-51D 44-13392/A 'Fabasca V' in the 339th Fighter Group at Fowlmere, Cambridgeshire in 1944. (via Ian McLachlan)

Incredibly, the Group claimed 239½ enemy aircraft destroyed in the air and 440½ on the ground for the loss of ninety-seven Mustangs. It was also the only fighter group to claim over 100 ground strafing victories on two occasions. The first was on 4 April 1944 (105) and the second was on 11 April (198).

P-51D 44-15074 'Big Noise' D7-J in the 503rd Fighter Squadron, piloted by First Lieutenant Dennis B. Rawls, which crashed on take-off from Fowlmere on 15 March 1945. (Dennis B. Rawls via Ian McLachlan)

The 339th Fighter Group left Fowlmere in October 1945 and the Ministry of Works retained the airfield until 1957 when the land was sold back to the former owners. E. F. Sheldrick & Sons Ltd of Manor Farm and the remainder bought the major part to Mr. F. Pepper of Black Peak Farm. In 1975 the Sheldrick family re-clad the T2 hangar.

Goxhill (Station 345)

This airfield was built close to the south bank of the Humber opposite Kingston-Upon-Hull and opened as a bomber station on 26 June 1941, later being transferred to Fighter Command. From August 1942 until March 1945 Goxhill, or 'Goat Hill' as it was known by the Americans, was used as a fighter operational training base. The first to arrive was the 52nd Fighter Group and in December 1943 the 496th Fighter Training Group was formed with two squadrons, one specializing in P-51 Mustang training and the other with P-38 Lightnings. Both Eighth and Ninth Air Forces were served by this establishment. The airfield was transferred to RAF Fighter Command on 20 January 1945.

Halesworth (Holton) (Station 365)

This airfield was built in 1942–43 with a standard 2,000-yard main runway and two others both 1,400 yards long, with fifty-one hardstandings and two T2 hangars and Nissen hut accommodation for 3,000 personnel. Though designated originally as a bomber station, the airfield was ideal for escort fighter operations; being located only eight miles from the Suffolk coast. In July 1943 the 56th Fighter Group commanded by Colonel Hubert Zemke arrived from Horsham St. Faith with eighty P-47 Thunderbolts.

A month after their arrival, on 17 August, the 56th were one of four P-47 groups detailed to escort the Regensburg force. The 'Wolfpack' picked up the rear box of bombers near Antwerp and stuck with them to Eupen before having to turn back. Although some interceptions of enemy aircraft took place no conclusive results were obtained. First Lieutenant Gerald W. Johnson fired at a Bf 109 before it eluded him. The P-47s returned after another disappointing flight.

On their second mission of the day, the 56th Fighter Group relieved the 353rd on schedule after taking off from Halesworth at 1520 hours and they met the B-17s returning from Schweinfurt near the Dutch border as briefed. Colonel Zemke wanted to penetrate as deeply as he could safely go and as with the morning raid, he deliberately chose to cross the enemy coast at around 20,000ft on a direct line from Halesworth. The 'bathtubs' were dropped as the P-47s passed near Antwerp and while they continued a steady climb. With the extended range provided by their auxiliary fuel tanks Zemke led his 'Wolfpack' 15 miles beyond Eupen, reminding his wingmen to swivel their heads regularly to see that they were not jumped by the enemy fighters. Visibility was unlimited. At 27,000ft Zemke spotted black specks in the deep blue ahead 'like a swarm of bees'. They were Fortresses

Pilots from 63rd Fighter Squadron. Standing, L-R: Captain Dave 'The Silver Fox' Robinson, IO; Al Davis; Handley Sayers, Flight Surgeon. Front: Gordon Batdorf; Walt Moore; James Peppers; Ray Petly; Wilfred Van Abel; Glenn D. Schiltz Jr and John Vogt Jr. On 11 January 1944 First Lieutenant Schiltz downed three Bf 109s to take his final score to eight. First Lieutenant Vogt scored the first of his eight victories on 19 August 1943 when he downed an Bf 109. (56th Fighter Group WWII Assoc via Alan Hague)

On 26 November 1943 the Wolfpack claimed twenty-three enemy fighters and this famous photo shows sixteen pilots presumed to be the victors that day. L-R: Captain Walter V. Cook (two Bf 110s); Lieutenants Stanley Bixby 'Fats' Morrill (Bf 109); John P. Bryant (Bf 110); John H. Truluck (Fw 190); Captain Walker M. 'Bud' Mahurin (three Bf 110s); Lieutenant Harold F. Comstock (Bf 110); Lieutenant Colonel Dave Schilling (two Fw 190s); Major (later Colonel) Francis S. 'Gabby' Gabreski (two Bf 110s); Captain Ralph Johnson (two Bf 110s); Major James C. Stewart, Group Operations Officer (Do 217); Lieutenants Frank W. Klibbe (Bf 109); Jack D. Brown (Fw 190); Eugene O'Neil (½ Bf 110 with Mark K. Boyle); Raymond Petly (who did not score); Flight Officer Irvin E. Valenta (two Bf 110s) and Lieutenant Anthony Carcione (Me 210). Lieutenant Fred J. Christiansen, who destroyed a Bf 110, is absent, which may explain why Petly took his place in the line-up. Morrill was killed when bombs aboard a 93rd Bomb Group Liberator, one of two which collided near the 56th Fighter Group base at Raydon on 29 March 1944, exploded during the brave rescue attempt to save the crew. Morrill had nine confirmed victories at the time of his death, the last on 16 March when he shot down an Fw 190 near St. Dizier. (56th Fighter Group WWII Assoc via Alan Hague)

and most of the enemy fighters were at the same level and as usual they were orbiting a few miles ahead prior to making a 180° turn to attack the combat boxes head-on. This gave the Thunderbolt pilots the advantage of being able to make diving attacks on the enemy fighters before they reached the B-17s especially since there did not appear to be any top cover for the Bf 109s and Fw 190s ganging up on the Fortresses. Zemke shot down a Bf 110 from 300 yards with a short burst. The next instant a body came hurtling out of the 110 and passed under his Thunderbolt.

In February 1944 the 56th Fighter Group at Halesworth became the first 8th Air Force Fighter Group to use nose colours for identification. There is, however, no mistaking the wolf insignia on Lyle Adriense's T-bolt, which of course refers to Zemke's famous 'Wolfpack'. The 56th Fighter Group flew Thunderbolts throughout the war, the only Fighter Group to do so, and the 'Wolfpack' even eclipsed all the Mustang groups by destroying more enemy aircraft in combat than any other. (56th Fighter Group WWII Assoc via Alan Hague)

The initial P-47 bounce had completely surprised the Fw 190 pilots who were not expecting to be attacked from the rear. In all the 56th Fighter Group claimed seven Fw 190s, four Bf 109s and five twin-engine fighters shot down in the lengthy combat. *Ritterkreuzträger* Major Wilhelm-Ferdinand 'Wutz' Galland *Kommandeur*, II./JG 26 disappeared from the action. Galland's remains were discovered two months later, buried with the wreckage of his Fw 190A-5. At the time of his death 'Wutz' Galland had flown 186 combat sorties, during which he had scored fifty-five day victories. He may have been the victim of an attack by Captain Walker 'Bud' Mahurin, who was credited with two Fw 190s. These were the first of 20.75 victories Mahurin would score before he was shot down on 27 March 1944. He returned to Allied control on 7 May but he was not allowed to fly

Barney Casteel survived the war, only to be killed in combat in Korea. (Alan Hague)

combat in Europe. Flying F-86E Sabres in the Korean War Mahurin destroyed three MiG-15s and he was also credited with a half share in a MiG kill as well as one 'probably' destroyed.

Two days later when the Group used similar tactics to claim another nine fighters Gerald Johnson notched a single kill making him the 56th Fighter Group's first ace. Johnson eventually scored a total of 16½ aerial victories and he was detached to fly with the 356th Fighter Group in November 1943 before being shot down on 27 March 1944 by ground fire and taken prisoner.

On 11 December 1943 when the heavies went to Emden, Captain Robert A. Lamb in the 61st Fighter Squadron, scored a triple victory which took his total to four. He scored three more victories in 1944 to take his final wartime score to seven. Lieutenant Paul A. Conger of Piedmont, CA also of the 61st Fighter Squadron, destroyed three enemy aircraft and damaged another. He finished the war with eleven confirmed victories.

On 6 February 1944 the 61st Fighter Squadron claimed three Bf 109G-6s of JG 26 shot down north-east of the Paris area, where the enemy pilots were about to pounce on the Fortresses. South of Paris a 56th Fighter Group P-47 shot down an Fw 190A-6 flown by *Oberleutnant* Artur Beese, *StaffelKapitän* 1./JG 26. Beese, who had scored twenty-two victories in 285 combat sorties, tried to bale out but he was killed when he struck the tail of his 190.

On 16 March 740 B-17s and B-24s went to factory and airfield targets in Germany and 679 of the bombers bombed Augsburg, Ulm, Gessertshausen and Friedrichshafen. The *Luftwaffe* was

P-47D-2-RA 42-22537 LM-T at a remote dispersal at Halesworth in Suffolk where the 'Wolfpack' was based from 8 July 1943 until 18 April 1944 after the more plush facilities at Horsham St. Faith early in 1943. LM-T was flown by Major Leroy A. Schreiber. (USAF)

up in force and twenty-three bombers were shot down. III/ JG 2 and all three Gruppen JG 26 converged on the B-17s at Nancy-St. Dizier where the 56th Fighter Group *en route* to support Fortresses on their way to Friedrichshafen, also came on the scene. The Thunderbolt pilots claimed eleven victories including three Fw 190A-6s and a Bf 109G-6 of JG 26. All four pilots were killed. Gabby Gabreski was credited with two victories, as was Fred Christensen, who had joined the 62nd Squadron as a replacement in the late summer of 1943. Zemke's 'Wolfpack' returned home with an 8:1 ratio of aerial victories to losses; by far the best in 8th Fighter Command.

In April 1944 Zemke's 'Wolfpack' left for Boxted in Essex, to make way for the 489th Bomb Group equipped with B-24 Liberators. (See *2nd Air Division Airfields*). The airfield was finally closed for flying in February 1946. Most of the land was returned to agriculture and in 1963 a large turkey farm was established on the runways by Le Grys, later Bernard Matthews Ltd, in January 1976.

Colonel Hub Zemke, one of the great US fighter leaders of WWII admiring his wing guns for the benefit of the camera. (USAF)

Captain Walker M. 'Bud' Mahurin, 63rd Fighter Squadron is congratulated by Captain Robert S. Johnson, 61st Fighter Squadron after another victory, which he scored flying P-47D-5-RE 42-8487 'Spirit of Atlantic City N.J.' Mahurin was shot down in this aircraft on 27 March 1944 but he evaded and returned in May. His 20.75 victories in WWII included 19.5 flying Thunderbolts. The other victory was in the PTO when he destroyed a Japanese Dinah flying a P-51D. (USAF)

P-47D-1-RE 42-7880 HV-N 'Redondo Beach, California', flown by First Lieutenant Paul A. Conger of the 61st Fighter Squadron. None of his 11½ victories were scored flying this particular Thunderbolt. (USAF)

Captain Robert Samuel Johnson, 61st Fighter Squadron, in the cockpit of his P-47D HV-P, which has twenty-five victories painted below the cockpit, the last two being Fw 190s for 13 April 1944. Johnson, who scored two more victories flying this aircraft on 8 May 1944 to take his score to twenty-seven, had racked up nine victories in 1943 flying different P-47s including P-47C 41-6235 'All Hell' and P-47D 42-8461 'Lucky'. Others included 'Half Pint (Pappy Yokum)', 'Double Lucky' and 'Penrod & Sam' (named for him and his crew chief Sergeant J. C. Penrod). (USAF)

Honington (Station 375)

This airfield was in use by the Eighth Air Force for a longer period than any other airfield in the UK, mainly being used as a maintenance base. It was turned over to the USAAF in the summer of 1942 and became an air depot for the major overhaul of aircraft. (See *Airfields of the 3rd AD*). Honington was used as an operational fighter base by the 364th Fighter Group from February 1944 to April 1945. The Group initially operated P-38 Lightnings (until July 1944) and then converted to P-51 Mustangs, the aircraft using hardstandings and blister hangars on the opposite side of the airfield to the air depot.

P-38J Lightnings of the 383rd Fighter Squadron, which operated them at Honington from February to July 1944. (USAF)

America and England have been described as two countries divided by a common language as Lieutenant Curtis Smart from Honington found out one night. "I had gone to a party in Cambridge and had left late. I was scheduled to fly the next morning and didn't dare miss a combat mission. I got into a taxi and told the driver to take me to Honington. I went to sleep and when the driver woke me and said we had arrived I found we were in *Huntingdon*! He'd misheard my southern accent."

On 28 February 1944, the 364th Fighter Group CO, Lieutenant Colonel Frederick C. Grambo, accompanying a 20th Group mission to gain operational experience, crashed near Zwolle in Holland and he was killed. The first of 342 operations by the 364th Fighter Group began on 3 March 1944. The unit was awarded a Distinguished Unit Citation for defence of bombers over Frankfurt on 27 December. The 364th Fighter Group flew their last mission on 25 April 1945 and departed for the USA in November. Meanwhile, Honington became US 8th Air Force Fighter Command HQ in October 1945. By the beginning of 1946, Honington remained the only active base of all the 122, which had been occupied by the Eighth Air Force. On 26 February a ceremony was held to mark its closure and official

P-51 N2 'Shack Lassie' N2-O in the 383rd Fighter Squadron. The 364th Fighter Group was awarded a DUC for their action on 27 December 1944 when they claimed 29½ enemy fighters that were massing to attack the bombers bound for Frankfurt. Captain Ernest Bankey became an 'ace in a day' with 5½ victories. (USAF)

handing back to the Royal Air Force. Brigadier General Emil Kiel, chief of Eighth Fighter Command handed over the keys of the base to Air Marshal Sir James Robb, AOC RAF Fighter Command.

Horsham St Faith (Norwich) (Station 123)

This pre-war built all-grass airfield near Norwich (See *WWII Airfields in Norfolk*) with five C-type hangars, permanent brick and tiled buildings with central-heating and a high standard of domestic accommodation was taken over by the USAAF in September 1942. The first occupants were the 319th Bomb Group (M) equipped with B-26 Marauders, who left for North Africa by the end of the year. On 5 April 1943 the 56th Fighter Group arrived from Kings Cliffe to begin fighter missions with their P-47 Thunderbolts. During the afternoon of 8 April a four-plane flight led by Colonel Hubert 'Hub' Zemke and four pilots in the 78th Fighter Group flew to Debden to take part in a 'Rodeo' set up by the RAF. The combined force of twenty-four P-47Cs penetrated 12 miles into enemy territory and returned after 90 minutes without seeing any enemy fighters. Zemke, Major Dave Schilling and two flight commanders in the 62nd Squadron, Captains John C. McClure and Eugene O'Neill, stayed on at Debden to gain further operational experience. A few days of unsettled weather however kept them on the ground until the morning of 13 April when all three Fighter Groups flew a 'Rodeo' to St. Omer in the Pas de Calais with the aim of luring the 'Abbeville Kids' into combat. Again the *Luftwaffe* fighters failed to show. That same evening another sweep was laid on and this time Loren G. 'Mac' McCollom and Phil Tukey brought a flight each from Horsham St. Faith to rendezvous with Zemke's flight at Debden before they all set off to fly as the third squadron in the 4th Fighter Group formation. Zemke was forced to abort over southern England with a faulty oxygen supply. Dave Schilling took over the 56th lead and followed the 4th Fighter Group to Le Touquet and out ten minutes later near Dunkirk where they were greeted with a few bursts of flak. Captain Roger Dyar suffered a complete engine failure over Dunkirk but from 31,000ft he was able to glide 25 miles across the Channel to belly-land near Deal. A burnt out ignition harness was found to be the cause of engine failure.

On the evening of 15 April the 4th put up twelve P-47s and the 56th and 78th each put up twenty-four Thunderbolts for another sweep of the Pas de Calais. They received a radio warning of enemy aircraft to the west of them and when a swarm of fighters suddenly appeared from that direction, the P-47 pilots thought they were in for a fight but it was another Thunderbolt group. By this time the 56th Fighter Group aircraft were scattered and they made their own way back to Horsham St. Faith and a lecture on air discipline from Hub Zemke. Inexperience cost the Group dear on 29 April when 112 P-47s of the 4th, 56th and 78th Fighter Groups flew another high altitude 'Rodeo' over the enemy coastline sweeping over the coast from Ostend to Woensdrecht. The thirty-six P-47s in the 56th Fighter Group, which were led on this occasion by Dave Schilling, took off from Horsham St. Faith soon after midday. Climbing at around 700ft a minute they headed for the enemy coast south of Flushing, where they were briefed to turn north and come out

Major Loren G. McCollom in front of a P-47. (Patty Bauchman)

near The Hague. Once the group had passed 20,000ft Schilling discovered that his radio was faulty. Instead of turning back and handing over to one of the squadron leaders, he chose to continue in defiance of standard operating procedure. While still over the sea and about 15 miles from Blankenberge, the briefed point of landfall Fw 190s of the 6th and 8th *Staffeln* JG 26 dived down out of the sun from 24,000ft and attacked the

Major Loren G. McCollom in front of his P-47 'Butch', at Horsham St. Faith in 1943. (Patty Bauchman)

leading 62nd Squadron from dead ahead. Schilling was unable to direct his squadrons or call for assistance and as a result the 61st Squadron flying top cover was at first unaware of the battle. When it was it waited for the radio call that never came. The flights became scattered and many pilots were unaware of what was happening and were at a loss to know what to do. Flying in pairs the Fw 190s swept in firing short, well-aimed bursts before diving away. *Unteroffizier* Wilhelm Mayer of the 6th *Staffel* claimed a P-47 30km north of Ostend and *Oberleutnant* Hans Heitmann of the 8th *Staffel* destroyed a P-47 at Knokke. By the time the coast of England was regained fuel was so low that many Thunderbolt pilots in the 56th Fighter Group had to land at the first airfield they saw. Schilling's fighter was one of three that returned to Horsham St. Faith badly damaged.

On 4 May when the 56th Fighter Group helped provide fighter escort up to 175 miles for the bombers attacking targets in Belgium Colonel Hub Zemke led thirty-four P-47s in support of the force of B-17s over Antwerp and shepherded them to the coast. Over Antwerp Zemke saw two Fw 190s diving towards the B-17s. He made a 180° diving turn to pursue the enemy but somehow he lost them. However, shortly he noticed four Fw 190s about a mile to his left. Zemke called for a left turn and gradually got himself in a position behind them; they were flying a string formation apparently oblivious to the P-47s' presence. Zemke singled out one of the Fw 190s. His first burst missed and his second burst produced a flash on top of the FW 190's canopy. His fire on both passes was too high. The 190 immediately rolled over into a dive but as he passed across his sight Zemke gave him a third burst and flashes appeared along the left wing root and fuselage before the e/a disappeared from sight below. Back at Horsham St. Faith Zemke found out that another flight in the 61st Squadron, which he had been leading had attacked other Fw 190s and made probable and damaged claims. Zemke was relieved to learn that all his P-47s had returned safely.

On the evening of 12 June Loren McCollom took the 56th Fighter Group on another sweep over the Pas de Calais. They went in at 20,000ft, far below their usual altitude. McCollom figured that the *Luftwaffe* always expected the Americans to be up around 30,000ft and might be caught off guard at a lower level. A *Staffel* of Fw 190s was seen about 5,000ft below while over Belgium. Schilling's flight went down to attack and McCollom took a long deflection shot at an Fw 190 as they broke and dived. Captain Walter Cook of the 62nd went down on some Focke-Wulfs that were trying to circle round and coming up behind the last man he held his fire until around 300 yards away and then let fly. His first shots struck the fuselage and then as prop wash caused his plane to veer slightly his fire began going into the enemy's left wing. A large puff of black smoke indicated he had hit the ammo compartment and a large piece of wing came off. Cook broke off the attack and pulled away. The Fw 190 was seen going straight down in an uncontrolled spin. As the enemy pilot took no evasive action it seems likely Cook's opening burst killed him. Zemke recorded in his memoirs, 'At last the 56th had made its first confirmed kill! At the same time I couldn't help speculating that at the current rate of attrition it would take a hundred years to decimate the *Luftwaffe*.'

Zemke had to wait until 13 June when he scored his first kills. During the morning and afternoon the short-ranged P-47s were used on two diversionary sweeps off the Belgian coast. In the morning the 56th Fighter Group came upon 10./JG 26. Over Dixmuide Zemke claimed two of the Fw 190s and one damaged.

On 26 June forty-seven P-47s of the 56th Fighter Group led by the Flying Executive Major Loren G. McCollom took off from Manston, Kent to provide withdrawal escort for B-17s that had bombed Villacoublay. The Thunderbolts proved too much of a temptation for *Hauptmann* Wilhelm-Ferdinand 'Wutz' Galland and his II/JG26 pilots. Galland led his fighters down out of the evening sun from 23,000–26,000ft and concentrating attacks on the 61st Fighter Squadron flying at 24,000ft, completely surprised the P-47 pilots from behind. Before they knew what had hit them Galland fired on one P-47 to the left of the formation and observed cannon strikes. He fired a second burst from the side and behind at about 50 metres and the Thunderbolt exploded. Parts of the wing, fuselage and tail flew off and the fighter dived away out of control and burst into flames. Galland did not observe the crash because he believed its destruction was certain and he attacked a second Thunderbolt. In all, five P-47s were shot down without loss and a sixth came down in the sea off Scratby. Lieutenant Robert S. Johnson in the 61st Fighter Squadron flying '*All Hell*' had a fortunate escape when an Fw 190, which pursued him and pumped 20mm shells into his Thunderbolt, was forced to break off out of ammunition. With a wave and a shake of the head, the German pilot rocked his wings in salute and broke off, perhaps thinking that the stricken P-47 would never make England anyway. Johnson however, managed to put down safely at Manston. Captain Gerald W. Johnson's claim for one enemy aircraft destroyed (the first of his 16½ victories) was confirmed. Zemke's leadership became more severe, which did not endear him to many of his pilots. New formations and tactics were experimented with during the operations of early July, but it was clear that altitude advantage was the key to success with the Thunderbolt.

The 56th Fighter Group's stay at Horsham St. Faith ended abruptly for they moved to Halesworth on 8 July to permit construction of tarmac runways to allow Horsham St. Faith to be used by Liberators of the 458th Bomb Group. (See *Airfields of the 2nd AD*).

King's Cliffe (Station 367)

Built as a grass airfield and as a satellite for Wittering for two fighter squadrons on dispersal, Kings Cliffe received its first American units in December 1942 when a few P-39 Airacobras in the 347th Fighter Squadron arrived for a short stay. In January 1943 the 56th Fighter Group, which had begun receiving P-47s in June 1942, arrived to learn RAF fighter control procedures and to train with P-47C Thunderbolts as these became available. Hard-surfaced runways and a perimeter track were laid down early in 1943 by W.&C. French Ltd. The length of the three intersecting runways were 1,100 yards, 1,700 yards and 1,325 yards, the longest being set on an E-W axis. Station offices were to the west of the airfield close to the village of King's Cliffe while the administration and technical area was to the east. A number of blister type hangars were erected for covered maintenance. Underground storage for 36,000 gallons of aviation fuel was provided.

During their sojourn at King's Cliffe Colonel Hubert Zemke, the CO arranged for his squadrons to carry out aerial gunnery with tow-target aircraft and range facilities at Llanbedr on the coast of Wales and at Matlask near the Wash in Norfolk. As the facilities were limited each squadron was sent for a period of two weeks. At Matlask a flight of P-47s would take turns in trying to hole the sleeve towed by a Lysander up and down a range over the sea. Matlask had no spare accommodation so the pilots were billeted in a nearby pub, which had a large flour grinding wheel implanted in the floor. The pilots called it the Wheel House, which seemed appropriate as Zemke was in attendance (officers were termed 'big wheel's). The weather was fairly good while they were at Matlask, whereas the 61st Squadron that went to Llanbedr could rarely get off the ground because of persistent cloud and rain.

Anthony Ralph Carcione (left), a pilot in the 62nd Fighter Squadron, his mother, and friend, Byron Morrill during leave, Christmas 1943, the last time his mother saw her son. Carcione was KIA on 8 March 1943 over Belgium when he was shot down flying P-47D-1-RE 42-7937 'Triss'. His body was brought back home to the USA in 1949 and laid to rest with a military funeral in Wind Gap, PA. His parents, Basil and Elizabeth, took their grief to their graves. (56th Fighter Group WWII Assoc via Alan Hague)

In April the 56th Fighter Group moved to Horsham St, Faith near Norwich to begin flying missions and Kings Cliffe did not receive another American Group until the following August when the 20th Fighter Group arrived with P-38H Lightnings.

Portrait of Colonel Mark E. Hubbard, 20th Fighter Group CO by Colonel Ross Greening in Stalag Luft I. Hubbard was shot down on 18 March 1944.

Accommodation was in short supply so initially, the 55th Fighter Squadron was based at Wittering and only returned when additional barracks had been built. The 20th Fighter Group began flying missions from Kings Cliffe on 28 December 1943 and it converted to the P-51 Mustang in July 1944.

On 28 January 1944 when fifty-four B-24s were despatched to France and came under attack from enemy fighters, P-38 Lightnings in the 20th Fighter Group appeared on the scene and JG 26 were forced to break off their attacks and seek cover in the clouds. The Lightnings shot down three of the Fw 190A-6s – killing all three pilots – while a fourth Fw 190A-6 flown by *Leutnant* Klaus Kunze of 2nd *Staffel* JG 26 was shot down by a 20th Fighter Group P-38 or a P-47 from another Group. (Kunze, who was WIA, baled out safely. He was KIA on 16 March 1944 when a 78th Fighter Group P-47 shot him down. See *Duxford entry*). The 20th Fighter Group lost two of their number to *Leutnant* Hans Hartigs of 2nd *Staffel* and Gefreiter Manfred Talkenburg of the 8th *Staffel*.

The 20th Fighter Group claimed 212 aircraft destroyed in the air and 237 on the ground and was awarded a DUC for the 8 April 1944 sweep over Germany. In all, the Group lost 132 fighters while at King's Cliffe. Their 312th and last mission was flown on 25 April 1945 and the Group began returning to the USA in October. The RAF took over the base and used it for armament storage until it was abandoned on 1 January 1959.

Leiston (Theberton) (Station 373)

This airfield, less than three miles from the Suffolk coast, was constructed in 1943 on 500 acres of land mostly in the parish of Theberton, by which name the airfield was also known. The dispersed camp site was to the west of the flying field, 2¼ miles from Saxmundham, the main runway was 2,000 yards long and the two subsidiary runways were each 1,400 yards long. The airfield's location made it ideal for fighter operations and the first unit to arrive, in November 1943, from Goxhill in Lincolnshire, was the 358th Fighter Group, which was equipped with P-47D Thunderbolts. The Group flew its first mission on 20 December but only flew a total of seventeen combat missions before transferring to the Ninth Air Force. They moved to Raydon at the end of January 1944 to swap places with the 357th Fighter Group, which was the first Group to be equipped with the P-51 Mustang. The 357th Fighter Group flew their first combat mission on 11

Captain (later Major) John A. Storch, CO 364th Fighter Squadron, with Asst. Crew Chief Sergeant Joe Kubarek and P-51D 44-13546 C5-R 'The Shillelagh', one of two Mustangs which had this name. Storch finished the war with 10½ victories. (Merle Olmsted via Ian McLachlan)

P-51D 44-13887 'Little Joe' with ground crew. (USAF)

February. On 5 March 1944 their second CO, Colonel Henry R. Spicer, was shot down and taken prisoner. The group's Mustangs were distinguished by red and yellow striped spinners and red and yellow chequerboard nose markings.

A Distinguished Unit Citation was awarded to the group for defence of bombers on missions to Berlin and Leipzig on 6 March and 29 June 1944. A second DUC followed for a mission to Derben on 14 January 1945 when the 357th had the highest claim for enemy aircraft destroyed on a single mission. The escorting Mustangs included the red- and yellow-nosed P-51s

In October 1944 Major Joseph E. Broadhead returned to Leiston as the Group Operations Officer. During the period from February to 28 May 1944 the 24-year-old pilot had scored six victories in the 362nd Fighter Squadron, which he commanded from 10 March 1944. Broadhead added two more kills to his victory total before being promoted Lieutenant Colonel in February 1945 and completing his second tour. (Merle C. Olmsted)

On 14 January 1945 161 enemy fighters were shot down. The 357th Fighter Group destroyed an incredible 60½ of them, a record, which stood until the end of hostilities in Europe. (The 20th Fighter Group claimed 19½ and the 353rd Fighter Group, nine). The CO, 27-year-old Lieutenant Colonel Irwin H. Dregne in P-51K-5 44-11678 'Ah Fung Goo/Bobby Jeanne' damaged one Fw 190 and shot down a Bf 109 25 miles north-west of Brandenburg. Dregne finished the war with five confirmed victories; he flew jets in the Korean War and died on active duty on 18 September 1967 at Selfridge AFB, Michigan. (Merle Olmsted via Ian McLachlan)

On 14 January 1945 Captain Leonard K. 'Kit' Carson in the 362nd Fighter Squadron at the controls of P-51K-5 44-11622 G4-C 'Nooky Booky' IV shot down two Fw 190s and a Bf 109. Carson finished the war with 18½ victories plus three Me 262s damaged. In the last year of the war the 357th Fighter Group had the highest scoring victory rate of all the groups and produced forty-six aces. (Merle C. Olmsted)

Captain Robert W. 'Father' Foy who on 29 June 1944 shot down two Bf 109s and an Fw 190 to take his score of victories to six enemy destroyed. Foy, who finished the war with fifteen victories, was killed in a B-25 crash in March 1950 near Phoenix, Arizona. (USAF)

Captain John B. England (22) (2nd from right) of the 362nd Fighter Squadron shot down four Fw 190s flying P-5ID-10 44-14709 G4-E 'Missouri Armada' on 27 November 1944, to take his personal score to sixteen confirmed victories in the ETO. His final total was 17½ kills. England was KIFA in an F-86F Sabre at Toul, France on 17 November 1954. (via Merle C. Olmsted)

Portrait of Colonel Henry R. Spicer, 357th Fighter Group CO by Colonel Ross Greening in Stalag Luft I. *Spicer was shot down on 5 March 1944.*

of the 357th Fighter Group commanded by Colonel Irwin H. Dregne. In the past eleven months the veteran group had flown 252 missions (most of which were bomber escort) and its pilots had been credited with 517 victories. No less than thirty-nine pilots had attained ace status. All told, the 357th shot down 60½ enemy aircraft a record for any 8th Air Force fighter group which still stood by the end of hostilities in Europe, for the *Luftwaffe* never again met the American fighters on equal terms.

The 357th Fighter Group flew their 313th and last mission on 25 April 1945. During this time they were one of the most distinguished Mustang outfits, with the second highest total for enemy aircraft destroyed in the air (609½) by an Eighth Air Force fighter group. They also destroyed 106½ aircraft on the ground. In July 1945 the 357th Fighter Group left Leiston for Germany where it formed part of the air forces of occupation. Leiston airfield was returned to the RAF on 10 October 1945.

Little Walden (Hadstock) (Station 165)
This airfield on a hill is partly in Hadstock and was a Class A airfield built in 1943. It was assigned to the Ninth Air Force Bomber Command in October and was the base for the A-20G Havoc-equipped 409th Bomb Group (Light) from March to September 1944. The base was transferred to the 8th Air Force and on 26 September the 361st Fighter Group arrived from Bottisham. Next day 1st Lieutenant Victor Bocquin, who was leading the 376th Squadron, claimed three Fw 190s destroyed while 1st Lieutenant William 'Bill' Rockafeller Beyer was credited with five Fw 190s. Credited with a total of eighteen German aircraft destroyed in the air and another three on the ground, the 376th Squadron had set a temporary record among the fighter groups of the 8th Air Force for enemy aircraft destroyed by a single squadron on a single mission. One 361st pilot – 2nd Lieutenant Leo H. Lamb – died when he collided with an Fw 190.

The yellow-nosed Mustangs operated from Little Walden until Christmas 1944 when the Group was one of two 8th Air Force P-51 units, which moved to the Continent to provide support for the beleaguered American armies in the Battle of the Bulge. On 26 December fourteen Mustangs in the 361st Fighter Group flew their first mission from St. Dizier with a sweep near Trier Göttingen at 17,000ft. They met a dozen Fw 190D-9s led by Oberleutnant Hans Hartigs of the 4th *Staffel* JG 26 and the 376th Fighter Squadron executed a diving turn to catch the German formation from behind. "We turned on them and they broke into us," reported First Lieutenant George R. Vanden Heuvel, who was flying tail-end Charlie in '*Mary Mine*'. Vanden Heuvel took on an Fw 190D-9, (Dora) which was attacking his element leader and he hit the Dora square on with a 20° deflection shot and it dived into the ground. The P-51D pilot then zoomed up looking for more enemy fighters and he saw down below an Fw 190D-9 chasing a P-51. The Dora was being flown by Hans Hartigs and the formation leader, who was out of ammunition, was flying the P-51. Vanden Heuvel closed to 200 yards and gave Hartigs' 190D a burst of fire. The fighter half-rolled and Hartigs baled out when his oil pressure dropped and his canopy filmed over with oil. Vanden Heuvel was credited with one Fw 190 destroyed to take his personal score to five and another shared with Captain Jay W. Ruch. In all, six Doras were claimed shot down (five were actually lost) without loss, one of the victims falling to Lieutenant Claire P. Chennault.

Some Mustangs and the ground echelon of the group remained at Little Walden until early February 1945 before joining the rest of the 361st, which moved from St. Dizier, France to Chievres in Belgium on 15 February 1945. At Little Walden during March 1945 the air echelon of the 493rd Bomb Group used the base while repairs were carried out on their runways at Debach. On 9 April the 361st returned to Little Walden to fly further fighter operations, the last on 20 April. Late that summer the 56th Fighter Group shared the base with the 361st Fighter Group before the base was relinquished by the 8th Air Force in November 1945 and the two groups left for the USA. Thereafter Little Walden became a store for surplus military vehicles before finally closing on 1 May 1958. Closure of the base allowed the B1052 Hadstock to Saffron Walden road, which had been closed when the airfield was built, to be reopened.

Martlesham Heath (Station 369)

Martlesham Heath aerodrome was first used as an aerodrome in the 1914–18 war. In 1917 it became associated with experimental aircraft and was later the home of the Aircraft and Armament Experimental Establishment. The A&AEE moved to Boscombe Down on 1 September 1939 and Martlesham became a Fighter Command station. In 1943, the station became one of a group of grass-surfaced airfields earmarked for use by fighters of the 8th Air Force and 1,600-yard runways were laid down using a then experimental process of soil stablisation with oil and tar products. Nearby housing estates and a major road presented difficulties in siting the runways and it was necessary to take the southern end of the NW-SE one through the middle of the camp. Aircraft hardstandings were both macadam-surfaced and steel mesh track. On 5 October 1943, the 356th Fighter Group, which was equipped with P-47D Thunderbolts, arrived from Goxhill. At first, Martlesham was shared with RAF units, notably Air

P-47D-6-RE 42-74702 of the 361st Fighter Squadron. Captain Sidney Hearst Hewett flew this aircraft in combat during early 1944 and he was finally shot down in air combat with six Bf 109s/Fw 190s on 4 May 1944. Hewett deadsticked his 'Jug' down between the Steinhuder and Dummer lakes: he came to a rest only inches short of a very large hardwood tree and was taken prisoner. Note the three victory symbols and Hewett's personal nose art; his black Labrador retriever dog 'Clarkie' carrying a Dornier Do 217 bomber in its mouth. The 356th Fighter Group changed to the P-51D Mustang in November 1944. (Dr. Jan Heitmann)

Major (later Major General) Donald J. Strait in the 361st Fighter Squadron on the wing of P-51D 44-15152 QI-T 'Jersey Jerk'. Strait scored 10½ of his 13½ victories flying P-51s.(USAF)

Sea Rescue, but with only limited accommodation available in the brick and timber barrack buildings, the US pilots had to be billeted in requisitioned country houses in the vicinity.

The 356th Fighter Group flew its first combat mission on 15 October 1943 and the 413th and last on 7 May 1945. During that time the Group lost 122 aircraft and claimed 201 aircraft in the air and 75½ on the ground. On 25 February 1944 when the

USSTAF brought the curtain down on 'Big Week' JG 26 claimed two 356th Fighter Group Thunderbolts and three bombers before starting on the stragglers. *Oberfeldwebel* Alfred Heckmann destroyed one of the Thunderbolts and *Hauptmann* Karl Borris, CO of I./JG 26 claimed a second but this P-47, though seriously damaged, reached England safely. On 16 March *Unteroffizier* Heinz Gehrke of the 11th *Staffel*, JG 26 who was flying a Bf 109G-6 on his first combat sortie and had just shot down a 458th Bomb Group Liberator (*Downwind-Leg*) found himself all alone. He tried to join some fighters in the distance but they turned out to be Thunderbolts of the 356th Fighter Group. The P-47s broke and Gehrke made the fatal mistake of trying to out-dive the pursuing P-47s and his Messerschmitt was ripped to shreds. He baled out and was fortunate to suffer nothing worse than a strained back.

On 23 April 1944 the 356th Fighter Group's second commanding officer, Colonel Einar A. Malstrom was shot down and taken prisoner. The Group was considered the hard-luck fighter group of the Eighth Air Force with a comparatively high loss-to-victories-claimed ratio, although the 356th was awarded a Distinguished Unit Citation for support given to the airborne landings in Holland on 17, 18 and 23 September 1944.

The Group converted to the P-51D Mustang in November 1944 and these were distinguished by red engine cowlings with a pattern of blue diamonds. Among the Group's aces was Major (later Major General) Donald J. Strait in the 361st Fighter Squadron, who scored 10½ of his 13½ victories flying P-51s. Captain Gerald W. Johnson, the 56th Fighter Group's first ace, was detached to fly with the 356th Fighter Group on 29 November 1943 to help the group during their introduction to combat. Flying with the 360th Fighter Squadron, on 24 January Major Johnson destroyed an Fw 190 and damaged another NE of Ypres to take his score to 8½ victories. He returned to the 56th Fighter Group in February 1944 and had scored a total of 16½ aerial victories when he was shot down on 27 March 1944 by ground fire and taken prisoner. In later years he rose to the rank of lieutenant-general in the USAF and commanded the 8th Air Force during the Vietnam War.

The 356th Fighter Group left Martlesham in October/ November 1945 to return to the USA. The Air Ministry finally relinquished the station on 25 April 1963. Today it is almost unrecognizable as an airfield, having become an industrial and dormitory town for Ipswich. A new road crosses the airfield and on the southern side of the road is a housing estate known as Martlesham Heath Village Hamlet. Suffolk County Constabulary is also headquartered here and the huge British Telecom Research Centre is on the north-east side just behind the old RAF technical site.

Metfield (Station 366)

When John Laing & Son Ltd built this airfield in 1943 the B1123 road running from Halesworth to Harleston had to be closed off so that the three intersecting concrete runways, fifty dispersal points and two T2-type hangars could be built. Temporary buildings were added on farmland to the south-west and eventually the base would accommodate 421 officers and 2,473 enlisted personnel as it was intended for use as a bomber base. However, the first American arrivals at the airfield on 3 August 1943 were the 353rd Fighter Group – the fourth Thunderbolt unit to join the Eighth Air Force – which arrived from the training airfield at Goxhill and were equipped with P-47D Thunderbolts. The Group began flying combat missions from Metfield on 12 August. Four days later the CO, Lieutenant Colonel Joseph A. Morris, was lost in action. Major Loren 'Mac' McCollom Flying Executive Officer of the 56th Fighter Group was loaned to lead the 353rd Fighter Group on 17 August when the 8th Air Force flew the double strike mission on Schweinfurt and Regensburg. Brigadier General Frank O.D. 'Monk' Hunter, chief of VIII Fighter Command, insisted the 353rd's operational advancement would be accelerated under an experienced leader and that neither the 4th or 78th Groups had anyone he rated as highly as McCollom. He saw a formation of Bf 109s 2,000ft below at 24,000ft and dived on them unseen. He fired a burst of .50 calibres at the rear aircraft flown by *Oberfeldwebel* Heinz Kemethmüller of the 7th *Staffel*.JG26, an experienced pilot who had made his debut in the west in December 1940 and had

Portrait of Colonel Loren G. McCollom by Colonel Ross Greening in Stalag Luft I. Major Loren 'Mac' McCollom Flying Executive Officer of the 56th Fighter Group was loaned to lead the 353rd Fighter Group on 17 August 1943. Next morning Colonel Hubert Zemke had orders rescinded for Mac's transfer to the 353rd Fighter Group, permanently. On 25 November 1943 McCollom was shot down and taken prisoner.

scored seventy victories on the Eastern Front. McCollom scored many hits and saw 'sheets of flame' and he was able to claim the 353rd Fighter Group's first victory. Kemethmüller was saved by his armour plate and when he reached low altitude he baled out near Leopoldsburg. His final score was eighty-nine aerial victories in 463 combat sorties.

Next morning Colonel Hubert Zemke had orders rescinded for Mac's transfer to the 353rd Fighter Group, permanently. On 25 November 1943 McCollom was shot down and taken prisoner. He was succeeded by Colonel Glenn E. Duncan, who on 7 July 1944 was shot down. Duncan evaded capture and commanded the 353rd Fighter Group for a second spell in 1945. During his time with the 353rd Fighter Group Duncan scored thirteen of his 19½ aerial victories. Another top scoring pilot in the group was Captain, later Major, Walter C. Beckham, who was the top scoring Eighth Air Force fighter pilot with eighteen aircraft destroyed at the time of his loss in combat on 22 February 1944. Beckham survived and became a PoW.

On 14 October 1943 when the Fortresses went to Schweinfurt over Walcheren Island more than twenty Bf 109s and Fw 190s, zooming in from over 34,000ft attacked the 1st Division. The Thunderbolt pilots stood their ground and met the attacks at around 31,000ft a height at which the Thunderbolt had the advantage over the enemy fighters. At a point between Aachen and Duren, the 353rd Fighter Group, at the limit of their range, was forced to break off and return to England. They had done their job well, beating off a succession of attacks and claiming ten fighters shot down and another five damaged or destroyed for the loss of one P-47 in combat and another which crashed in England on the return leg.

On 30 December 1943 the 8th journeyed to the IG Farbenindustrie chemical works at Ludwigshafen, on the upper Rhine near the German-Swiss border. The German controller expected a raid on Paris so he ordered II./JG 26 and the 4th *Staffel*, I/JG 3 south. *Fähnenjunker-Feldwebel* Gerd Wiegand inadvertently led the 4th *Staffel* into the middle of the 353rd Fighter Group formation. South of Florennes, Belgium Wiegand got on the tail of one of the P-47s, flown by First Lieutenant William 'Dub' Odom in the 350th Squadron and shot him down. Odom was killed. The 353rd Fighter Group broke up an attack by Bf 109s of I/JG 3 that had been sent south when an attack on Paris was expected. Two of the Bf 109s were shot down but the 353rd Fighter Group lost its second P-47 when an unseen enemy shot down Second Lieutenant Russell E. Moriarty in the 352nd Fighter Squadron. Moriarty baled out and he was taken prisoner.

On 21 January while flying at 17,000ft west of St. Quentin a flight of P-47s in the 353rd Fighter Group spotted four Bf 109s flying south-east just above the cloud tops. Major Walter Beckham and the rest of the flight opened their throttles and nosed down, closing easily. Beckham picked out the Bf 109G-6 flown by *Feldwebel* Hans Oeckel and fired at him from less than 200 yards astern, getting many strikes and setting the Messerschmitt on fire. Oeckel quickly baled out and landed safely east of Laon-Sissonne with facial burns and a slight concussion. It was Beckham's 12th victory and his 13th soon followed. Beckham opened fire on another 109 to the right as he was breaking left. Range was so short that hits resulted in spite of the deflection. He followed this Bf 109 down in a series of manoeuvres with throttle full back and turning so sharply that he was stalling most of the time. Beckham thought his quarry was also stalling. The electrical sight went out after the first burst at the second 109. Using the mechanical gunsight

Beckham gave him a burst each time the 109 straightened out. His canopy and miscellaneous pieces came off but Beckham did not think that the pilot got out before the fighter broke apart. The American ace watched one of his wings with a piece of fuselage attached, spiralling down flaming. When it struck the ground it started a large circular area burning. Beckham's second victim was *Oberleutnant* Erich Burkert; an experienced pilot with two victories in seventy-one sorties, who had he lived would have been promoted to *Staffelführer*. Walt Beckham scored his 18th and final aerial victory on 8 February 1944. He was shot down by flak 14 days later and taken prisoner.

Colonel Glenn Duncan, the 353rd CO, reached the conclusion that a squadron, specially trained in the art of ground strafing, would be an ideal weapon and Metfield was selected as the base for the new unit. On 18 March 1944 volunteers from four fighter groups assembled under the command of Colonel Duncan and became the 353rd 'C' Fighter Group at Metfield where a mock target was erected to practice strafing tactics and manoeuvres. The new unit soon became known as 'Bill's Buzz Boys' after General William Kepner who had agreed to establish the unit. However, on 12 April 1944 the 353rd transferred further south to Raydon and Metfield became a heavy bomber airfield again when the B-24 Liberators of the 491st Group arrived on the base. (See *Airfields of the 2nd AD*). The base was returned to the RAF in 1945 and subsequently abandoned. The airfield was sold during 1964–65 and Metfield was returned to agricultural use.

Mount Farm (Station 234)

Originally a grass field and satellite for the RAF Photographic Reconnaissance Unit at Benson, in February 1943 Mount Farm was occupied by F-4 Lightning photographic aircraft of the 13th Photographic Squadron which commenced missions at the end of March. On 7 July 1943 the 7th Photographic Group (R) was established at Mount Farm to control the 13th, 14th, 22nd and 27th Photographic Squadrons. The 7th flew 4,251 sorties and it received a Distinguished Unit Citation for its work in covering the Normandy invasion. Mount Farm's grass field was replaced with a concrete runway, hardstands and taxiways and blister hangers were used to house the Spitfires and Mustangs. On 1 May 1945 the airfield was handed back to the RAF and finally sold in 1957.

Nuthampstead (Station 131)

Construction of Nuthampstead airfield was begun in 1942 in Scales Park on land owned by Baron Dimsdale by the 814th and 830th Engineer Battalions of the US Army. The base was laid out to the standard bomber field specification but in September 1943 the 55th Fighter Group with Lockheed P-38H Lightnings became the first American unit to occupy the base when they arrived to begin long-range escort missions for the bombers. The 55th flew their first combat mission on 15 October and thus became the first P-38 group of the Eighth Air Force to see combat. Missions from Nuthampstead were dogged with problems with the Lightning's Allison engines, which were affected by the humidity and extreme cold at high altitudes over north-west Europe and resulted in a high rate of attrition. In March 1944 the group's Lightnings became the first aircraft of the Eighth to fly over Berlin. Early in April the 55th Fighter Group moved to Wormingford to allow the B-17G Fortresses of the 398th Bomb Group to move in and become the third group in the 1st Combat Bomb Wing. (See *Airfields of the 1st AD*).

Raydon (Station 157)

A Class A standard bomber airfield, built by the 833rd and 862nd Engineer Battalions of the US Army in 1942–43, fighter units only ever used Raydon. The bomb-dump was situated in Raydon Great Wood to the north of the flying field. Dispersed camp sites, which in total could accommodate 2,842 men, were to the south-east and nearly all in the village of Great Wenham. The airfield received the 357th Fighter Group late in November 1943 when the base was Ninth Air Force command but the 357th Group swapped places with the 358th Fighter Group and its P-47 Thunderbolts at Leiston in late January 1944. The P-47s were already flying escort missions and they continued to do so even though transferred to the Tactical Air Force. In April 1944

353rd Fighter Group pilots at briefing at Raydon. (USAF)

the 358th moved to the south coast and Raydon was transferred to the Eighth Air Force with the arrival from Metfield of the 353rd Fighter Group, which was equipped with P-47s. Colonel Glenn Duncan, already a distinguished ace, commanded it. The Group was at the time one of the most successful P-47 groups in 8th Fighter Command.

The 8th Fighter Command provided support for the bomber missions on 12 June 1944 and attacked German communications and troop movements. For the 353rd Fighter Group it was their most disastrous mission of the war. At Raydon at 0434 hours Colonel Glenn E. Duncan took off and led forty-eight P-47s, each aircraft armed with 3,500 rounds of .50 calibre API ammunition and two 500lb bombs under the wings but no external fuel, to the airfield at Evreux/Fauville. Hits were scored on freight

Captain Walter C. Beckham, 351st Fighter Squadron, whose usual mount was P-47D-5-RE 42-8476 YJ-X 'Little Demon', finished the war with eighteen victories; all scored flying the Thunderbolt. At the time that he was shot down by flak and taken PoW on his 57th mission on 22 February 1944 he was the highest scoring American ace in Europe. (USAF)

cars parked in sidings and radar installations and adjacent barracks were also bombed with three direct hits and two near misses. The P-47s descended below the cloud level at 3,000ft and destroyed several trucks in a convoy in the vicinity of St. Saen before they were split up by light flak when they let down through the overcast. The remaining flight was forced to jettison their bombs as they were bounced by Bf 109s who flew out of the clouds and descended on the rear of the Thunderbolt formations in the vicinity of Dreux. The P-47 pilots dropped their bombs and belly tanks and went into a tight circle but they were out-turned by the enemy. In the furious aerial battle that followed the 353rd Fighter Group pilots claimed six Bf 109s but eight P-47s were shot down. Colonel Duncan claimed three 109s to take his overall score to 18.5 victories, at one point calling for help over the radio as he had six Bf 109s 'surrounded'! Colonel Duncan scored his 19th victory on 5 July and two days later he was shot down by flak NE of Nienburg in P-47D 'Dove of Peace VII'. He evaded and made his way to Holland where he remained with the Dutch underground until liberated on 14 April 1945 in Arnhem.

During 'Market-Garden' on 21 September only ninety P-47s of the 353rd (and 56th) Fighter Groups were able to provide escort and patrol support for the airborne forces. The P-47s of the 353rd Fighter Group reached the Nijmegen area in time to take on some of the attacking fighters of the IInd and IIIrd *Gruppen* JG 26 and the 'Wolfpack' claimed fifteen fighters shot down and one damaged. But the Fw 190s nevertheless shot down three transports. The 353rd Fighter Group claimed three Fw 190s destroyed and one probable and one damaged for the loss of one Thunderbolt in the 350th Fighter Squadron, led by Lieutenant Colonel Kenneth W. Gallup. He spotted thirty–forty Fw 190s and Bf 109s and engaged them from 9,000ft to the deck just south of Nijmegen. *Oberfähnrich* Otto Fussi of 6./JG26 was killed at Nijmegen when his Fw 190A-8 was shot down by a P-47 pilot. *Oberfähnrich* Günther Patzke of 9./JG26 was KIA when a 353rd Fighter Group P-47 pilot shot down his Bf 109G-6 at Groesbeek. Two other JG26 pilots who were flying Fw 190A-8s were WIA by 353rd Fighter Group P-47 pilots. *Leutnant* Wilhelm Hofmann CO of the 8th *Staffel* JG26 claimed a P-47 at Zwolle. The 353rd Fighter Group received a DUC for its actions during the 'Market-Garden' Operation. Lieutenant Colonel Gallup finished the war with nine confirmed aerial victories, all of them while flying the Thunderbolt.

In October 1944 P-51Ds with colourful yellow and black chequerboard cowlings replaced the P-47Ds. The 353rd remained at Raydon until October 1945 when the Group left for the USA. The Group had flown a total of 447 combat missions and had claimed 330½ aircraft destroyed in the air and 414 on the ground with 137 of their own aircraft MIA. Raydon was transferred to RAF Fighter Command on 20 December 1945, although no further flying units were stationed at the airfield. A small part of the airfield was sold in 1952 and the station closed officially on 8 August 1958.

Steeple Morden (Station 122)

This airfield began its existence in late 1940 as a small grass satellite for Bassingbourn three miles to the north-east and was expanded in 1941 with the addition of three runways built by John Laing & Son Ltd. The main E-W runway was 1,600 yards long and the two others, 1,100 yards and 1,075 yards each. Fifty-five concrete hardstandings were added and a T2 hangar and seven blister hangars were erected. The technical site was on the north of the airfield and dispersed living sites were built to the north-east to house 2,000 men. Late in 1942 USAAF photographic squadrons flying reconnaissance versions of the Lightning and Fortress, prior to being sent to North Africa in November used the base briefly. During this period Lieutenant-Colonel Elliott Roosevelt, CO, 3rd Photo Reconnaissance Group, commanded the base. In 1943 the airfield became an Eighth Air Force fighter base.

In May 1943 Steeple Morden was used by Blenheim Is of 17 OTU and then in July 1943 the 355th Fighter Group arrived

Major (later Lieutenant Colonel) Claiborne H. Kinnard Jnr, 354th Fighter Squadron CO. Kinnard scored eight victories flying Mustangs in the 355th Fighter Group. (Marshall via Crow)

Major James 'Jabby' Jabara who flew a second tour in the 354th Fighter Squadron in February 1945 and who became a jet ace in the Korean War flying F-86 Sabres. (via Crow)

with their P-47D Thunderbolts. In March 1944 the Group converted to P-51B Mustangs and later operated P-51D and P-51K Mustangs. Sharing the airfield from July 1944 was the 1st Scouting Force and later the 2nd Scouting Force, which flew reconnaissance flights ahead of the main bomber forces.

The 355th Fighter Group flew its first combat mission on 14 September 1943 and the last on 25 April 1945, flying over 17,000 sorties and having damaged or shot down over 1,500 aircraft in

P-51B 43-6431 'Man O' War' WR-A in the 354th Fighter Squadron in 1944 which Lieutenant Colonel Claiborne H. Kinnard was flying when he downed an Fw 190 on 29 March 1944 and two Me 410s and a Bf 109 on 7 July 1944. (via Crow)

Steeple Morden control tower. (Glynn Williams via Crow)

the air and on the ground. By the end of the war, the 355th held the record for the most enemy aircraft destroyed by ground strafing by the 8th Air Force. It was awarded a Distinguished Unit Citation for attacks on airfields in the Munich area on 5 April 1944 with most of the forty-three aircraft claimed destroyed and eighty-one damaged plus eight in the air) being obtained at Dorniers airfield of Oberpfaffenhofen.

On 28 January 1944 when fifty-four B-24s were despatched to France IInd *Gruppe* JG26 intercepted P-47s in the 355th Fighter Group. *Feldwebel* Wilhelm Mayer of the 7th *Staffel* was back in the air again at about 1220 hours and ten minutes later he shot down a 355th Fighter Group P-47. Mayer landed, topped up his tanks and rearmed before he took again with his wingman to look for more stragglers. *Unteroffizier* Erich Lindner of the 8th *Staffel* had meanwhile claimed another 355th Fighter Group P-47 20km east of Marche. In all the 355th Fighter Group lost four P-47s on 29 January.

On Friday 18 August 1944 all personnel on the base turned out in masses to see and hear Major Glenn Miller present a programme called 'The Moonlight Serenader' with his fifty piece American Supreme Allied Command Band. Only the

P-51B 42-106950 WR-P 'Iowa Beaut' (ex 'Man O' War') in July 1944. (via Crow)

most skeletonized crews remained at their jobs during this afternoon's performance. Twenty-five hundred enthusiastic GIs from the base plus others from nearby bases, including the 91st Bomb Group at Bassingbourn, sardine packed the big hangar on the flight line. Men were all about the hangar. Fifteen long rows of chairs and benches weren't enough. Every supporting girder held a capacity of swing fans. A few bolder ones sacrificed safety for 'look-see' by occupying high positions. Featuring musicians and big-name artists such as Sgt Ray McKinley, Drummer, who prior to this assignment led his own band; Sgt Carmen Mastren, Guitar, formerly with Tommy Dorsey; Sgt Johnny Desmond, Vocalist, formerly with Gene Krupa and Sgt Bobby Nichols, Trumpet, formerly with Vaughan Monroe. Augmenting these were a special twenty-piece string section of former soloists and members of the Philadelphia, Boston and Cleveland Symphonies. A quintet from Miller's last civilian band included Lieutenant Don Haynes, Miller's personal representative; S/Sgt Trigger Alpert, Base-fiddle; M/Sgt. Zeke Zarchy, First trumpet; S/Sgt Jimmy Priddy, First trombone and T/Sgt Jerry Gray, one of America's foremost arrangers.

General Carl 'Tooey' Spaatz and other officers at Steeple Morden in 1944. (Moseley via Crow)

Some of the numbers played by the band in a one hour programme featured favourite swing and novelty numbers such as 'Moonlight Serenade', 'Stardust', 'GI Jive', 'Tuxedo Junction', 'Cow-Cow Boogie' and 'Serenade for Strings'. The back centre stage was an innovation of two Air Force airplane trailers parked together on which were seated the fifty musicians. The stage was built up for Ray McKinley and his drums. On McKinley's left was the string section, and on his right, reeds and vocal section. After the performance, GI autograph hounds and photographers kept Major Miller and the band personnel busy posing for pictures. Later the musicians had supper with F-122ers and left in five Liberators for another engagement. Major Glenn Miller returned again on Saturday 26 August 1944 to the station Officers Club with a select group from his band and played for an officer's dance, with over 400 people attending the affair.

The first piggy-back rescue of a pilot in the ETO was accomplished on 18 August 1944. Captain Bert W. Marshall Jr.,

Bob Kunhert and 'Barny' Barnhouse enjoying a brew and doughnuts from the Red Cross Clubmobile at Steeple Morden. (via Crow)

commanding officer of the 354th Squadron, was leading his flight on a low level attack of German transport facilities North of Paris when his Mustang was hit by flak. He recalled: "It sounded like somebody had tossed a handful of gravel hard against my plane. The Mustang shuddered and I knew I'd have to belly it in." Marshall called over his radio to the members of his flight and told them that he had to crash land his flak riddled aircraft, which was also on fire. This act certainly meant captivity as a prisoner of war. Lieutenant Royce W. Priest, flying the No.3 position in the flight contacted Marshall on his radio transmitter; "Bert, I'm gonna find a road close by and land and pick you up. When you see me coming in, start running toward my plane." Priest landed in an adjacent grain field, clearing a path with his wings, taxied to his waiting commanding officer in a zig-zag pattern while Marshall displayed a bit of the open field running that won him acclaim as a former 1937–38 Vanderbilt College All-American football quarterback. During this time, the remaining members of the flight buzzed 50ft overhead to provide cover. Priest jettisoned his parachute and dinghy, tossing them out to make room for the stocky Marshall. Scrambling onto the wing, Marshall slipped under Priest and squatted down in the cockpit with his lanky

P-47 D YF-Q 'Damn Yank' in the 358th Fighter Squadron following an accident in November 1943. (Morris via Crow)

team-mate sitting on his lap. He called his rescuer a 'silly so-and-so', then the two manned the controls of the Mustang, taking off from an improvised runway, with Germans all round shooting at them, clearing a haystack by inches. Upon arrival at the home base, Priest asked for a straight-in approach. When he said that there were two pilots aboard, the control tower officer refused to believe him and stood in amazement. On the final approach to the runway Priest put the gear down and Bert lowered the flaps. The landing was uneventful, but a first for two pilots landing a Mustang. Priest turned onto the grass and taxied to the squadron operations rather than to the dispersal pads. Priest was awarded the DSC.

The last 8th Air Force shuttle mission was flown on 18 September when 110 B-17s escorted by 150 Mustangs dropped supplies to the Polish Home Army in the ruins of Warsaw. A total of 105 B-17s and the sixty-four Mustangs succeeded in reaching their shuttle bases at Mirgorod and Poltava. Captain Pete Hardiman, a P-51 pilot in the 354th Squadron, recalls:

On 18 September the 8th Air Force flew a shuttle operation, named 'Frantic 7' to help relieve Polish freedom fighters in

P-51 Club at Steeple Morden. (via Crow)

Warsaw, escorted by the 4th, 355th and 361st Fighter Groups. Unfortunately, most of the supplies fell into German hands. The B-17s made it to Poltava and Mirgorod. Our fighter base was Piryatin. On 19 September most of the fighters left Piryatin to rendezvous with the B-17s near Horodenka, Poland and crossed over Czechoslovakia, Rumania and Hungary and bombed their target near Brod, Yugoslavia. There was much heavy flak but we all made it to Italy, landing at Foggia. After a short rest we left Foggia on 22 September to rendezvous with the B-17s near Marseilles. All 355th aircraft were down at Steeple Morden by 1700 hours. This was the most awe-inspiring mission I ever took part in.

Looking back, Colonel William J. Hovde, 358th Fighter Squadron, remembered the Firth of Clyde when the 355th disembarked from the *Queen Elizabeth,* the long trip to Steeple Morden and the former RAF site that became his home for many pleasant months. He remembered too their Nissen hut quarters. British bikes with handlebar brakes, huts that made up the officers club with the great De Costa murals, the circular bar and 'Wild Bill's Mustang Blend Scotch' flown in via C-64 from Scotland to be bottled locally are a few of his early memories. How could

P-47D WR-M 'Gator Baby' in the 354th Fighter Squadron and Lieutenant Minchew. (Moseley via Crow)

P-51D 44-73144 'Man O' War' at Steeple Morden in 1944. (via Crow)

Children's party at Steeple Morden. (via Crow)

he forget his first short sweep when he first saw flak and the red roofs of Holland?

Later it was the thrill and fun of combat, forming up in terrible weather, waiting for the blower to cut in on the climb out, rendezvousing with the 'Big Friends', scoring my first victory, the smell of cordite, the sound of ripping metal when crashing, the shuttle raid to Russia and so many enemy aircraft over Berlin. How could anyone forget the

Staff Sergeant Moseley painting the kills on Lieutenant Charles Barger's Mustang in the 354th Fighter Squadron at Steeple Morden. (via Crow)

Captain Walter J. 'Korky' Koraleski Jr., in the 354th Fighter Squadron, the 355th Fighter Group's first ace with five kills 6 March to 5 April 1944. Koraleski was forced down with engine trouble over Holland on 15 April 1944 and taken prisoner. (via Crow)

P-47D 42-8434 WR-U 'Miss Behave/Lil Lo' painted by the famous 355th Fighter Group artist 'De Costa' who also painted several murals on walls on the base. (via Crow)

great music makers of the 355th who won all the contests in England? The musical talent of Price, De George, Nelson and so many others who proved that flying wasn't their only talent. How well I remembered the NCOs and airmen who kept us flying, crew chiefs who were closer than family.

P-51D 'Texas Terror IV' in the 355th Fighter Group at Steeple Morden. (via Crow)

Lieutenant Colonel Bert W. Marshall, CO of the 354th Fighter Squadron who on 18 August 1944 was picked up by Lieutenant R. W. Priest in the first piggy-back rescue of a pilot in the 8th Air Force. (via Crow)

Truly a great group of men! Lastly the pilots with whom I flew: Cummings, Stewart, Kinnard, Dix, Marshall, Graham, Ekstrom, Sluga, Hubbard, Gresham, Szaniawski, Elder and so many, many more.'

Lieutenant William J. Cullerton in the 357th Fighter Squadron remembers Sergeant Booth who 'mothered' the entire squadron and Father McHugh who helped many through some difficult times; the guys on the line who 'crewed' the planes and especially his chief Jerry.

> Lord how they babied those planes and worried, and then how they would run right out in front of the plane when you were still on the taxi ramp to see if the tape over the guns had been broken. I remember the ice coated wings, the foggy take-offs (sometimes the fog was internal), the bad, bad weather; my first sucker hole, the Flak. The time I strafed a silo and thought I'd knocked out a radar station. I remember the trip to Russia, we escorted the 'Big Friends' who dropped supplies to the incredible Poles, who were fighting the Russians in Warsaw and the Germans on the western edges. I remember the buzz bombs and the V-2s and the countryside around Litlington and Steeple Morden and the indomitable spirit of the British people who took many of us time and time again into their homes and shared rations, and gave us a touch of 'home'.

The base was returned to RAF Fighter Command on 11 November after the 355th moved to Germany for occupation duties in July 1945. The station was closed down on 1 September 1940 and abandoned.

Wattisham (Station 377)
Built in 1938 by John Laing & Son Ltd during the RAF pre-war expansion phase, Wattisham was originally a grass airfield. It had permanent technical and domestic accommodation and four C-type hangars on the eastern side of the airfield near the village of Great Bricett. In 1942 the airfield was turned over to the USAAF for use as an air depot and work started on building concrete runways for heavy bomber use. However, Wattisham remained an air depot and when it was planned to station a fighter unit here, work ceased on the runways and only the main runway and short stretches of the other two received a concrete surface. The main runway was finished off with steel matting while the taxiway and some additional hard-standings also received a concrete surface. In late 1943

Wattisham (officially named Hitcham) became the 4th Strategic Air Depot. An additional technical area with four T2 hangars, some eighteen hardstandings and a taxiway loop joining the airfield perimeter track, was constructed on the south side of the airfield. An engineering complex in temporary buildings was built around this area chiefly in the village of Nedging Tye.

The 479th Fighter Group with P-38J Lightnings arrived in May 1944 and soon became known as 'Riddle's Raiders' after the first Commanding Officer, Lieutenant Colonel Kyle L. Riddle who was shot down on 10 August 1944. He evaded capture and returned to the Group to take command once again on 1 November 1944. In the meantime, Colonel 'Hub' Zemke, who had 15.25 victories on P-47s, had taken command of the 479th Fighter Group and in late September the Group converted to the P-51 Mustang. Zemke scored two more victories and damaged another on 26 September, and received a half share in a Bf 109 kill on 7 October before he was shot down leading the Group on 30 October 1944 and taken prisoner.

A total of 351 fighter missions were flown from Wattisham. A pilot flying from this base made the last Eighth Air Force claim of an enemy aircraft destroyed during the war. Earlier, on 5 December 1944, Major Arthur F. Jeffrey in the 434th Fighter Squadron claimed three Fw 190s to take his score to nine. He would increase his score to twelve with a triple kill on 23 December and another victory followed on 25 December when he destroyed a Bf 109 SW of Bonn. With another Bf 109 destroyed on 14 February 1945 his final score reached fourteen confirmed victories.

On 9 February 1945 Major Robin Olds, 434th Fighter Squadron CO claimed three victories. Olds had scored five kills flying P-38 Lightnings in August 1944 before the 479th Fighter Group had converted to the P-51 that September. His first P-51 victory had come on 6 October 1944 when he shot down an Fw 190. Major Olds' claims for two Bf 109s and the Fw 190 destroyed on 9 February were confirmed and they took his score to ten. On 19 March Major Olds led sixteen P-51s in his P-51K and claimed a Bf 109 and an Fw 190 to take his score to twelve victories. Olds and his pilots made landfall between Knokke and Ostend at 14,000ft. They rendezvoused with the B-24s east of Strasbourg at 21,500ft and escorted them to, through and from the target to Creilsheim where the squadron broke from the bombers and swept the areas of Giebelstadt airfield, Kitzingen, Würzburg, Volkmarsen, Paderborn and Münster. While in the Münster area, twenty-five-plus Fw 190D-9s of JG26, who were assigned a mission to provide airfield cover for the Me 262 photo reconnaissance jets at Münster-Handorf, were sighted at 8,000ft. Bf 109s were also in the area. Having the advantage in the bounce after using the haze as cover during their approach Olds led his Squadron in the attack on the Fw 190s though Yellow Flight became separated as the squadron closed. Olds' nine P-51s engaged the Doras, which immediately went into a Lufbery to the left, pulling contrails as they circled at 13,000ft in the haze. Olds' Squadron joined in the Lufbery; gaining altitude as the pilots waited for the Germans to break. The Dora pilots performed barrel rolls, shallow 'split-esses' and other manoeuvres before pulling back up in an attempt to lure the P-51 pilots into following them down. Finally, as Olds reached the level of the enemy formation's leader the majority of the Fw 190s broke downward and the Mustangs attacked. An 8-minute dogfight ensued in which JG26 lost two Fw 190D-9s and a Bf 109. One P-51 pilot took a 20mm shell in his wing from a burst of fire by *Leutnant* Friedrich Ramthun but made it home safely. First Lieutenant Richard G. Simpson confirmed the Fw 190D-9 that Major Olds claimed: Olds destroyed a Bf 109 over the Dummer Lake on 7 April and he also damaged an Me 262, to take his wartime score to thirteen victories. He was credited with four MiG-21s shot down in combat during the Vietnam War January-May 1967.

One of the fighter pilots at Wattisham during the war was Clarence 'Buck' G. Haynes who as 'a country boy' had spent his youth in a small town in North Carolina so all of his time in England was one of 'enlightenment and pleasure'. He recalls:

I joined the Air Corps on 23 September 1942 and received my wings on 8 February 1944. After being trained as a fighter pilot, I arrived at Prestwick about 3 August 1944 and then went to Stone for a few days processing. Then it was to Goxhill near Hull for check out in a Mustang. I went to Wattisham about 1 September and was assigned to the 434th Fighter Squadron. It was a hell of an exciting time and learning just how war takes place was an eye opener. My first mission was Berlin on 28 September. I appreciated being lucky enough to live in permanent quarters with steam heat, 60ft to the mess and a beautiful lounge. There were Liberty Runs to Ipswich in the black out – hair-raising! – to attend movies. The first and subsequent trips to London were out of this world for a little ol' country boy. I had always been a people watcher so you could imagine me in London.

In February 1945 Haynes met his fiancée, Margory, a WAAF telephone operator at Earls Colne airfield in Essex.

We had a phone in the hall of our quarters and so our relationship grew. Soon we would meet each other at the bus station in Colchester, have a nice dinner at a quaint hotel on the High Street just above the Roman ruins, maybe see a movie and then back to Ipswich. We didn't date a great deal but when we had time off we would go to London and I would stay at Marge's home in North Finchley. Movies and sightseeing occupied most of our time. Learning more and more about English sacrifices was interesting. Marge's brother of my age had been killed on a bombing raid over Germany and was missing in action. He was recovered in Holland in 1958 or 1959. I would take a Mustang down to Marks Hall and spend a short visit. My departures would usually be a little smart Alec but the tower seemed to enjoy them. I also knew where Marge's hut was so I gave them an occasional 'low pass'. I was able to take Marge up in a jump seat of a worn out Mustang, which was quite interesting. I believe that very few Mustang jocks have had the opportunity.

The war ended. I had completed my tour prior and had started a second tour. We were notified that we would go to

Japan so I volunteered – until the big blast in Japan. We were having a weekend party and Marge was visiting a second time. I went to my boss and suggested that as Marge was in the RAF there should be no restriction on her flying in our planes. We had a war weary Mustang which by removing an 80 gallon fuel tank behind the pilot plus a couple of electronic items, there was sufficient room for a passenger to squeeze in and sit on a makeshift seat. All agreed that Marge could fly and I fitted her into a flying suit and she climbed aboard, big dimples, rosy cheeks and all! Or plans were to fly over Earls Colne and maybe to North Finchley. Foolishly and rather stupidly, I revved the engine up, let go of the brakes roared down the runway, held it low to the ground long after reaching take off speed and then proceeded to pull up sharply in a chandelle. That was the beginning, We levelled out and headed for Earls where I began to circle so that she could get a good view. I could talk to her but she could not talk to me. Soon she was tapping me on the shoulder and motioning a return to Wattisham. It required no great imagination to see that she wasn't doing well. I smartened up, flew gently back, made probably the smartest landing in my career but taxiing in, she could resist no longer but she did a magnificent job in not 'exploding'. When the crew chief climbed up to the cockpit he looked at her face and remarked that, it "looks like you left your roses upstairs". Marge quickly remarked, "That's not all I left".

Our unit was headed for home and discharge but I wanted to fly and stay in. luckily four of us were able to get assigned to the continent and later to an airfield in a suburb of Munich.

I continued to correspond with Marge. Married couples were rapidly filling up the base and fraternization was taboo. So one thing led to another and before I knew it she had talked me into hitching. England was planning to celebrate Battle of Britain day on 15 September 1946 and a contingent of aircraft from our base was to participate. However, I was only a spare pilot so we decided it would be a pretty good time to tie the knot. We had four days to arrange a marriage.

I left for Neubiberg about ten miles from Munich but Marge had to go through the usual red tape to procure a military pass etc and so started married life in a country we had just been at war with. It was an experience. However, we both survived!

So too has Wattisham. It continued in front line service with the RAF until fixed wing operations ended at the airfield on 31 October 1992 and the Army Air Corps moved in during July 1993 and have been flying helicopters from the station ever since.

Westhampnett (Station 352)
This airfield, now Goodwood aerodrome was used by Spitfire Vs of the 31st Fighter Group from 1 August until 21 October 1942, the first combat mission being flown on 29 August. The Group was assigned to 12th Air Force Fighter Command on 14 September 1942 but it continued flying missions under the command of 8th Fighter Command until 10 October that same year. During its short stay in England the 31st Fighter Group, which had flown P-39 Airacobras in the USA, was the first complete USAAF group to become established in the UK. Its greatest action from Britain was during the ill-fated Dieppe operation on 18 August when the 31st Fighter Group flew 123 sorties over the French beaches. Lieutenant Samuel S. Junkin was the first pilot in the American Air Forces thus far in the war to claim a victory when he shot down an Fw190 before being shot down himself. He was rescued but the 31st Fighter Group lost eight Spitfires over Dieppe. Until the Group left for North Africa they escorted bombers and protected RAF ASR aircraft.

Wormingford (Station 159)
Richard Costain Ltd built this airfield in 1942–43 partly in the parish of Fordham and incorporating a WWI landing ground used by aircraft operating against Zeppelins. Originally designated as a standard Class A heavy bomber airfield, the layout included a 2,000-yard main runway on an E-W axis and two intersecting runways of 1,400 yards each. Fifty hardstandings and two T2 hangars, one each side of the

Ground crew working to clear the snow off a 343rd Fighter Squadron, 55th Fighter Group P-51D Mustang at Wormingford. (TAMM)

airfield, were also built and eventually accommodation for 421 officers and 2,473 enlisted personnel was constructed in dispersed sites to the south and east of the airfield in and around Fordham village. However, Wormingford proved surplus to Eighth Air Force bomber requirements and the airfield was re-designated as a fighter base. The 55th Fighter Group which was equipped with P-38H Lightnings, arrived from Nuthampstead on 16 April and remained until the end of hostilities. The group ended the war with claims for 316½ enemy aircraft destroyed in the air and 268½ on the ground, losing 181 aircraft missing in action.

Eager fighter pilots were mainly disappointed that D-Day, 6 June 1944 did not provide a rich hunting ground for *Luftwaffe* targets. The P-38s were given the job of covering the ships in the Channel because not even the most trigger-happy ack-ack gunner on the ships could mistake the twin-tailed Lightning. Five squadrons of Lightnings flew cover all the time over the ships. Robert P. Tibor was disappointed at first because the clouds were low and they could not see far. It did not look like 'the show' was so big after all but as the limited horizon unrolled he kept seeing ships, ships and more ships. Big and little ships were spread from England to within 15 miles of the French coast, creeping under the cloud cover as darkness came. Out in front were the destroyers, cruisers and battleships and behind moved the concentration of troop and supply ships. In all Tibor was aloft on three occasions and on the last one at 5 o'clock the weather was improved enough for him to see the water off the French coast. The coast was 'black' with ships and landing craft and he thought it looked like 'the jam at Piccadilly Circus on a Saturday afternoon'.

Another P-38 pilot in the Group, Robert P. Tibor, saw an Me 109 carrying bombs and dived for him but somebody else got him. He didn't last long. The only other enemy plane he saw was another '109, which dived out of the clouds. Three Spitfires screamed into view after him. The '109 swooped down toward the water and up into the clouds again, the Spits right on his tail. Over the beachhead Tibor saw streams of tanks 'crawling in' like 'an invasion of beetles'. He also saw gliders that had carried men 'lying all over the landscape'. Some gliders were broken. The ground was spotted with coloured parachutes, which had dropped guns and supplies. Like most others he thought 'Jerry' would throw up every plane that 'would get a wheel off the ground' and it was just a milk run for the Allied fighters. Coming back he saw a big ship concentration moving out of the Thames estuary behind a smoke screen.

The 55th converted to P-51 Mustangs in July 1944 and adopted yellow and green chequerboard nose markings as identification for its aircraft. Late in 1944, the 3rd Scouting Force was formed at Wormingford, operating Mustangs and, later, a few Fortresses.

On 29 August 1st Lieutenant Walter J. Konantz in the 338th Fighter Squadron, flew his 12th mission after arriving at Wormingford. He had flown his first combat mission on 8 August when the group escorted the B-17s to Romilly-sur-Seine airfield south of Paris. The majority of Walt Konantz's thirteen combat missions during August included some spectacular ground strafing and dive bombing of targets in France and Holland. On the 29th he was one of the 55th Fighter Group pilots who strafed train targets just over the French border into Germany. He recalled:

> I was 2nd or 3rd man on most of the train strafing. I shot up three trains, one of which was a long troop train. The train was moving fast when I raked it from the rear to the front and I saw soldiers jumping out of the windows while it was still moving at 30–40mph. When it finally stopped, I saw 50–60 people lying in the fields and ditches near the tracks. Another train made it safely into a tunnel and would not come out. Lieutenant Lanham shot down a Do 217 and I saw it crash.

On 11 September raids cost forty-five B-17s and B-24s. It was also the biggest air battle of the war for the 55th Fighter Group, whose fifty-two Mustangs escorted the 3rd Air Division B-17s to Ruhland. In the 338th Fighter Squadron 1st Lieutenant Walter J. Konantz, who was flying his 17th combat mission, recalls:

> Just before rendezvous with our bombers we were climbing through 24,000ft and I had to get rid of my second cup of coffee. To use the relief tube in the P-51 it was necessary to undo the lap belt, unsnap the leg straps of the seat type parachute, then scoot well forward on the seat to use the relief tube, which was a plastic cone attached to a rubber tube which vents overboard out the belly of the plane. It was stowed on a clip under the seat. I was completely unbuckled, sitting on the front edge of my seat when a voice came over the radio, "109s, here they

come". About fifty Me 109s had bounced our squadron and about fifty more engaged our other two squadrons up ahead. Just a few seconds after the warning on the radio, a single Me 109 passed directly in front of me in a 45° dive. With a reflex action, I peeled off after him. He evidently saw me as he steepened his dive to the vertical. I firewalled the throttle and steepened my dive to match his. During this wide open vertical dive our speed increased to near compressibility, both airplanes were as skittish as a colt on a wooden bridge, As I was vertical and virtuously weightless, the slightest movement of the stick would cause me to leave the seat and be stuck against the canopy. A very slight pull on the stick would put me back down in the seat. I felt like a basketball being dribbled down the court as I bounced back and forth between the canopy and the seat. Just before I started a careful pullout at about 8,000ft, I saw the airspeed needle bumping 600mph – 95mph over the redlined airspeed of 505mph. Holding a steady 4G pullout, I regained level flight at about 3,000ft. Meanwhile, the 109 was bouncing around and appeared pretty unstable and hard to control at that speed. He started to pull out of his dive about the same time I did but was not successful. His right wing buckled through the wheel well area and he spun into the ground with a fiery explosion. The pilot had no time to get out. I claimed a 109 destroyed and what confirmed the claim was that after the massive 20 minute dogfight, one of the 55th Fighter Group pilots reported that he counted thirty fires on the ground, which would account for the twenty-eight Me 109s claimed and the loss of two Mustangs. I never got close enough to the 109 to fire my guns and I was too excited to think to take gun camera pictures of the impact point. My plane had only a few popped rivets, which speaks well for our beloved P-51 and its equally dependable Merlin engine. I would also compliment the sub contractor who made the sturdy canopy.

On 1 January First Lieutenant Walter J. Konantz flew his forty-eighth combat mission when the Wormingford group escorted the B-17s to Derben oil refinery near Stendal. Konantz recalled:

Lieutenant Walter Konantz and his younger brother, 2nd Lieutenant Harold Konantz both of the 55th Fighter Group. Walt flew P-51D 44-72296 CL-P No.6, which Lieutenant Colonel John McGinn had named 'Da Quake' (he downed four enemy aircraft in CL-P) and he flew it until his last mission on 6 October 1944. At this point the Mustang was taken over by Walt Konantz who renamed it 'Saturday Night.' It carried him through a full tour, flying over sixty combat missions without a mechanical abort. All four of Walt Konantz's kills were in this Mustang. Walt flew his last mission on 23 February 1945 and CL-P No.6 was taken over by his brother Harold, who had just arrived as a replacement pilot. He left the name 'Saturday Night' and had only to change the rank and first name on the canopy tail. On 7 April 1945 he was flying his 7th mission when he was hit by gunfire from the side turret of a B-17. He lost his coolant and the engine caught fire forcing a bale out. He was a PoW for the remainder of the war. CL-P No.6 ended in a fiery crash 50 miles north-west of Berlin. (Walt Konantz Collection)

Lieutenant Bodiford got hit by flak and baled out over France. He came back a few days later carrying his wadded up parachute. My girlfriend made Bodiford and me an aviators scarf out of it and a pair of panties for herself. On this mission we saw a couple of airfields with parked German planes but they laid a curtain of flak over them too thick to try to strafe.

On 6 January seven fighter groups flew escort and one group strafed airfield and transportation targets First Lieutenant Walter J. Konantz flew his 50th combat mission this day when the Wormingford group escorted the B-17s to Germerscheim. Konantz recalls:

> We strafed Germerscheim airfield on the way out and the 338th Squadron got thirteen aircraft destroyed. I got a Ju 88, which was slow catching fire, but when I looked back it was starting to burn. Captain Buskirk was hit by flak from the airfield and baled out. Lieutenant Ramm was badly damaged by flak but he made it back to base. He had to belly in at 200mph as battle damage made his plane uncontrollable below this speed.

Walt Konantz had taken part in an uneventful P-51 escort for the B-17s to Bielefeld on 7 January but the 13th January, during a freelance area support mission, instead of its usual bomber escort missions, was a day he would remember for the rest of his life. He not only recorded his third kill but it was the first claim for an Me 262 by the 55th Fighter Group. Following correspondence with Lorenz Rasse and Herr Boehme in 1986 Walt Konantz learned that the pilot of the Me 262 (Werke Nu. 110601 9K+EH) was *Unteroffizier* Alfred Färber of 1./KG 51 another former bomber unit that was converting to the jet aircraft at Giebelstadt. Färber was on an acceptance flight following maintenance and repair work on his Me 262. Konantz flew his 53rd and 54th missions on 21 and 22 January when the 55th Fighter Group escorted the B-17s to Mannheim and Sterkrade. On the latter mission he and the rest of Red Flight closely escorted three crippled B-17s to the Dutch coast on the way home. On 29 January Walt Konantz notched his fourth aerial victory of the war when the 55th Fighter Group escorted the B-17s to Kassel and he shot down a Bf 109.

After the 55th Group left in July 1945 to take up duties with the occupational air forces in Germany, Wormingford passed to the control of the RAF.

Summary of Airfields and Other Locations

Ashby, Suffolk
Description: Memorials to USAAF fliers.
Location: Off unclassified road 1 mile North of Somerleyton.
Directions: Head for the church of Ashby St. Mary near Herringfleet Hall.
Comments: A stone in the churchyard is dedicated to the American airmen of the 100th Bomb Group killed 'near this place on 7 May 1944 and also on 8 April 1945 Lieutenant Russell P. Judd and Flight Officer Louis S. Davis, all of the U.S.A. 8th Army Air Force [sic] gave their lives in defence of this country. Greater love hath no man than this, that a man lay down his life for his friends.' First Lieutenant Ralph W. Wright and four of his crew in the 349th Bomb Squadron who died on 7 May 1944 are commemorated on the same memorial stone near the gate of the 13th Century church of Ashby St. Mary, as Judd and Davis of the 5th Emergency Rescue Squadron at Halesworth. During a mock combat their P-47Ds collided and crashed in Fritton Lake. Judd was flying P-47D-6-RE 42-74705 and Davis P-47D-15-RE 42-76175. An outer wing section was one of many relics recovered from the lake in 1971 and is now on display in the USAF Museum at Wright Patterson Air Force Base in Dayton, Ohio. (The story of these two incidents can be found in *Final Flights* by Ian McLachlan (PSL 1989))

Atcham (Station 342)

Description: American fighter base.

Location: In parkland north of the A5 and River Severn and 3 miles south-east of Shrewsbury.

Directions: Follow signs for Atcham Industrial Estate.

Comments: Though the runways have been broken up and removed and the control tower demolished, the three T2 hangars remain. As does the administration buildings, which form the Atcham Industrial Estate.

Berinsfield, Oxfordshire

Description: Memorial to USAAF fliers.

Location: Off A423.

Directions: Leave junction 7 on M40 motorway and head SW on the A329 to Stadhampton. Turn right on to B480 to Chislehampton, then left on to B4015 and go to A423. Turn left and go about a mile to the Berinsfield roundabout. Turn left into minor road and left again. Memorial and church are on the right.

Comments: A Spitfire propeller with spinner painted PR blue is fixed to a plinth in the village. The plaque beneath depicts the 8th Air Force and RAF badges and a Spitfire and Lightning, both of which flew from the nearby Mount Farm airfield. The inscription reads: 'In memory of those who served 7th Photo Group, the eyes of 8th USAAF, Mount Farm. 5,693 missions 1943–1945. Dedicated 25th May 1985.' The memorial was made in Florida and transported across the Atlantic to be erected in Oxfordshire. A Scroll of Honour can be found in Berinsfield church. Fields within the old aerodrome site are named after local wartime personalities. Weitner Field, appropriately incorporating much of the reclaimed main runway, commemorates Major Walter L. Weitner who, on 6 March 1944, flew the first Spitfire photo mission to Berlin.

Bodney (Station 141)

Description: RAF satellite airfield for RAF Watton in the early war years and later, a USAAF airfield.

Location: A Breckland site on the B1108 east of the A1065 Swaffham to Brandon road.

Directions: turn onto B1108 Watton road. Immediately after Bodney is the airfield, now a British Army camp.

Comments: Inside the main gate of the army camp, which now occupies the site of the wartime aerodrome, is a memorial, dedicated on 9 July 1983, to all who served with the 352nd Fighter Group. A Thunderbolt and a Mustang are shown on the memorial, together with the words: 'From these fields, American airmen joined their British allies in the cause of freedom.'

Bottisham (Station 374)

Description: American fighter base.

Location: In open farmland adjacent to the A45 Cambridge to Newmarket bypass.

Directions: For the lychgate, go down Tunbridge Lane.

Comments: In the Church of the Holy Trinity is a plaque, dedicated on 17 June 1984, bearing the words: 'In memory of the Airmen of the 361st Fighter Group US 8th Air Force who gave their lives in the defence of freedom 1943–1945.' An identical plaque was put into the refurbished control tower at

Statue of Liberty mural on a wall at Bottisham airfield in May 1981. (Author)

B-17 with a yellow-nosed 361st Fighter group Mustang and the words, 'Here's a toast to those who love the vastness of the sky' on a wall at Bottisham airfield in May 1981. (Author)

Little Walden, 10 miles south, on the same day. In Bottisham village in October 1986, a road in a new housing area being built was named in honour of Colonel Thomas J. Christian Jnr, who was KIA on 12 August 1944. The idea originated from a member of the 361st Preservation Group living near Bottisham and so 'Thomas Christian Way' was inaugurated. The colonel's daughter, Ms Lou Christian Wilson Fleming (44), whom he never saw, was flown from Texas by the building firm and took part in a naming ceremony at Bottisham on 16 October 1988. A jazz band played as a P-51 Mustang gave a display and there was a colour guard from the US Air Force. A lychgate at the entrance to the new housing area, where Thomas Christian Way begins, covers a plaque which was unveiled by Lou Christian. It reads: 'This Street is situated on what was part of Bottisham air base and is named in honour of Colonel Thomas J. Christian, Jnr, commander of the 361st Fighter Group, US Eighth Air Force, who, with members of his command, flew from here and gave his life in the defence of freedom during World War II. Unveiled by Colonel Christian's daughter, Ms Lou Christian Wilson Fleming, on 16 October 1988. Lest we forget.' The housing estate stands on the former communal site. American murals in war-time brick huts, showing the 8th Air Force insignia,

'Off we Go into the Wild Blue Yonder' on a wall at Bottisham airfield in May 1981. This brick mural is one of several that have been carefully and expertly removed over the past few years. It is now faithfully displayed at Thorpe Abbotts. Unfortunately, after removal, some brick murals (like the ones at Podington and Mendlesham) were inexplicably repainted (badly) and thereby rendered no longer authentic or historic. Unless the wrongly applied paint can be removed they are now really only fit for the skip. (Author)

the Statue of Liberty and other items, were removed and distributed between the IWM, Duxford, a US Air Force base and an aviation museum in the USA.

Two crew huts in a corner near the A1303 road are the only remaining buildings. The A45 Newmarket bypass was built across the site of the airfield. During the war the Officers' Mess was at Bottisham Hall, home of the Jennings family. Hutted accommodation was built nearby. Visitors should not enter the area with the huts, which is privately owned. Anyone wishing to see Bottisham Hall should first inform one of the local contacts: Mr Raymond King, 42 Vicarage Close, Swaffham Bulbeck, Cambridge CB5 0LY. Telephone 01223 811894. Mr Steve Gotts, 49 Edinburgh Road, Chesterton, Cambridge.

Boxted (Langham) (Station 150)
Description: American fighter base.
Location: 5 miles NE of Colchester, West of the A12.
Directions: Follow A12 and turn off onto B1066.
Comments: Very little remains of the airfield site.

City of Norwich Aviation Museum (CONAM) Old Norwich Road, Horsham St. Faith, Norwich NR10 3JF. Tel: 01603 893080
Description: Aviation Museum featuring the 100 Group Memorial Room and historical aircraft and exhibits.
Location: on the northern edge of Norwich International Airport (formerly RAF Horsham St. Faith), which offers a good view of the passenger aircraft flying from this expanding regional airport.
Directions: Leaving Norwich take the A140 towards Cromer and turn right off the bypass after the main airport entrance.
Comments: No trip to the region's airfields and tourist attractions is complete wtihout rounding everything off or starting with a visit to this museum, which was conceived and is run by a dedicated band of volunteers. A Vulcan bomber dominates the Museum's collection and a variety of other aircraft, both civilian and military, are also on display. Within the Museum's exhibition building are displays showing the development of aviation in Norfolk. There are special displays relating to the 458th Bomb Group and other units which served at the airfield during the war and after. The Stafford Sinclair Room is dedicated to the operations of 100 Group RAF (see *100 Group (Bomber Support) Aviation Heritage Trail*). An excellent gift shop sells books, models and other items. Opening Times: April to October: Tuesday to Saturday 10.00–5.00. Sunday and Bank Holidays 1200–5.00. School Holidays, 1200–5.00. November to March: Wednesday and Saturday 10.00–4.00. Sunday and Bank Holidays 12.00–4.00. Closed over Christmas and New Year. Admission prices vary. Children under five free.

Debden (Station 356)
Description: RAF and American fighter base.
Location: Two miles south-southeast of Saffron Walden on the southern side of the Thaxted road.

Directions: From M11 turn off at junction 9 and follow Saffron Walden to Thaxted road (B184).

Comments: On 18 October 1973 a Nissen hut, officially designated Building 210, which had been used by the 4th Fighter Group, was presented to the USAF to be flown to the Wright Patterson AFB in Ohio to be reassembled and displayed in the USAF museum. A bronze memorial plaque on a flower bed near the guard room is the sole reminder of the presence of the top-scoring 'Eagles' (4th Fighter Group) at Debden from September 1942 until after the war. Just inside the former main gate is a pillar recalling its distinguished past: 'RAF Debden was home of the 4th Fighter Group 8th Air Force US Army Air Force WWII from September 1942 to September 1945. Vanguard Yanks of the 71st 121st and 133rd RAF Eagle Squadrons and their Spitfires traded RAF blues for US Army olives to become the 4th Fighter Group. Long ranging Thunderbolts, later Mustangs, were to help a dedicated 4th Group achieve the most victories over enemy aircraft in the entire US Army Air Force. 1,016 enemy aircraft were destroyed. In remembrance of our comrades who were not to see the war's end and of Anglo-American endeavors to a common cause. We survivors of the 4th Fighter Group humbly dedicate this memorial.' It was unveiled on 11 July 1981. *(See also Saffron Walden)*

In Grosvenor Square, London, is an obelisk-type memorial to the Eagle squadrons. The inscription on the front says: 'This memorial is to the memory of the 244 American and 16 British fighter pilots and other personnel who served in the three Royal Air Force Eagle squadrons prior to the participation of the United States of America in the Second World War'. On an interior wall of the Battle of Britain Hall at the RAF Museum at Hendon, north London, is a frame containing an RAF badge for the three Eagle squadrons.

Duxford (Station 357)

Description: RAF and American fighter base, now the IWM Duxford.

Location: In a shallow valley to the east of the A505 Royston to Newmarket road.

'Counting the Cost' is a memorial sculpture in glass comprising 52 panels engraved with the outlines of aircraft, one for each plane MIA flown by the USAAF in WWII, designed by Renato Niemis for the American Air Museum. Some 7,031 aircraft are depicted and represent losses incurred by both the 8th and 9th Air Forces and the US Navy. It lines the route to the entrance to the Museum creating a striking and symbolic approach and a contemplative counterpoint to the interior of the American Air Museum. (Author)

Directions: Follow signs from M11 and A505.

Comments: Just inside the main gate of the airfield is a flat stone inscribed: '1943–1945 Erected by American Army Forces personnel to commemorate two years of combat operations against Nazi Germany while stationed at Duxford from 8 April 1943 until the Victory in Europe 8 May 1945. They destroyed 333 German aircraft in aerial combat and 343 while strafing airfields. This plaque is offered as a tribute to the courage of those airmen and to the devotion to duty of ground specialists

Duxford Control Tower in 1996. (Author)

whose work made these victories possible. 78th Fighter Group including Headquarters 82nd, 83rd and 84th Fighter Squadrons. 443rd Air Service Group including Headquarters and Base Services Squadron, 643rd Air Materiel Squadron and 819th Air Engineering Squadron.'

Duxford airfield in 1996. (Author)

Duxford airfield in 1996. (Author)

The Red Lion at Whittlesford was a favourite pub for RAF and USAAF pilots in WW2. Behind the bar is a framed photo of P-47 42-25871 'Nigger II' flown by Captain Richard M. Holly CO, 84th Fighter Squadron. The Thunderbolt was named after Holly's always-suntanned wife. (Author)

Grumman Bearcat owned by the Fighter Collection in a hangar at Duxford. (Author)

Early in January 1945 the 78th Fighter Group finally completed the changeover from Thunderbolts to Mustangs. First Lieutenant Hubert 'Bill' Davis, a 25-year old pilot in the 83rd Squadron had within days of his arrival, been allocated a newly-delivered P-5ID, which appropriately, he named 'Twilight Tear' after a legendary bay filly racehorse foaled in 1941 at the famous Calumet Farm in Lexington, Kentucky in the heart of America's horse racing industry. (Author)

167

The AirSpace Museum. (Author)

The magnificent AirSpace Museum at Duxford. (Author)

The AirSpace exhibition features twenty-five military and civil aircraft displayed both on the floor space and suspended as if flying. These rare and historic aircraft represent the story of British aviation through the 20th century. Alongside the collection of aircraft are interactive displays about aircraft, how they fly and how they are made. The interactive displays are fun

An EE Lightning of No. 74 'Tiger' Squadron and other aircraft in the AirSpace Museum at Duxford. (Author)

The American Air Museum, with, appropriately, a P-51D Mustang of the 78th Fighter Group. (Author)

The American Air Museum during Proms Night. (Author)

Duxford airfield in June 2006. (Author)

Duxford airfield in July 2007. (Author)

Captain Ben I. Mayo, acting CO of the 82nd Fighter Squadron who flew P-47D 42-26671 MX-X 'No Guts – No Glory!' destroyed an Fw 190 flying the original aircraft, on 20 June and on 1 July 1944 he damaged an Fw 190. He is credited with the destruction of four enemy aircraft while flying P-47s as acting CO of both the 84th and 82nd Fighter Squadrons during June to September 1944. (Author)

Renovation is a major part of the day to day work of the Fighter Collection at Duxford. Here the Gloster Gladiator is undergoing rebuild in 2006. (Author)

for all ages and every level of interest; AirSpace includes an area devoted to aircraft conservation, for which Duxford is world famous, where visitors can see vital conservation work taking place. The exhibition space also contains supporting displays of engines, vehicles, weapons and other items from the Imperial War Museum's collections. The 12,000 square metres of Airspace tells the story of British aviation from the early pioneering days through to what the future may hold. The displays are a mix of video and sound, items to handle, computers, words, pictures and hands-on displays. The first floor gallery is a superb way to view all the exhibits.

East Wretham (Station 133)
Description: American fighter base now an Army base.
Location: On unclassified road off A1075, 6 miles north-east of Thetford and three miles from the A11.
Directions: after Thetford join A1075 and turn left into minor road to East Wretham.
Comments: A plaque on the base of the East and West Wretham war memorial reads: This plaque commemorates the visit by survivors of the 359th Fighter Group in remembrance of those who served and died in the cause of freedom 3rd August 1985.'
(See also Thetford, Norfolk)

Fowlmere (Station 378)
Description: RAF and American fighter base.
Location: Off B1368 south of Cambridge, 3¼ miles north-east of Royston.
Directions: Between Royston and Duxford airfield on A505, turn into minor road to Thriplow and Fowlmere, on B1368. Go through the village and past the Chequers pub. Entrance to Manor Farm ahead.
Comments: A beautiful set of RAF wings painted on the wall of one of the buildings has been restored. A plaque shows the outline of the grass aerodrome of Fowlmere with its hangar and tower, and the positions of the 503rd, 504th and 505th Fighter Squadron dispersals. On it is superimposed a side elevation of a P-51 Mustang and the words 'Station F378'. The accompanying

inscription reads: 'The 339th FTR Grp 8th A.F. from April 1944 until October 1945 flew off the grass of Manor Farm to join our Allies in victory over Hitler's forces in Europe. To the American men and woman of this unit the village of Fowlmere gave the hospitality and support that made of those trying times a fond memory. Here was our haven in that war.

This plaque is dedicated to all who served in the 339th Fighter Group and its supporting units and to their tireless providing of the Mustang sorties launched from here in the allied cause of freedom. God bless all who knew those times and this place. 339 FTR GRP ASSN 1985.'

In addition, money donated by the 339th Fighter Group Association was used for the creation of a nature garden at Fowlmere County Primary School. A plaque on the wall reads: 'Nature's Classroom. In appreciation for the hospitality and support provided by the people of Fowlmere to the 339th Fighter Group, US 8th Air Force, during World War II. 339th Ftr Gp Assn 1986.'

The 339th's aircraft had red and white chequerboard nose markings and appropriately the Chequers pub in Fowlmere has a similar sign with a plate bearing the words '339 Fighter Group 1944 – Mustangs'. Photographs of the airfield and its aircraft are displayed inside the pub.

Goxhill (Station 345)
Description: American fighter base.
Location: On unclassified road 3 mile NE of village.
Directions: Leaving the M180 at junction 5 head north on A15 towards the Humber Bridge. Before the bridge turn east on to A1077 sand go through Burton-upon-Humber and in Barrow-upon-Humber take minor roads to Goxhill. Join Howe Lane and then Horsegatefield Road.
Comments: On the north-western perimeter of the old airfield is a stone cairn surmounted by a twisted propeller blade. The main plaque is inscribed: 'United States Army Air Force No. 345 Base Goxhill Fighter Training Group June 1942–February 1945. Gone, but not forgotten.' Two further plaques are fastened to each side of the cairn. One records that the memorial was erected by residents

Goxhill in 1997. (Michael Fuenfer)

of Goxhill and their friends, on behalf of USAAF personnel who served here, and that it was unveiled on 9 September 1984. The other explains that the propeller blade was recovered from the local crash site of P-38 Lightning 42-67199 of the 496th Fighter Training Group. The accident occurred on 26 May 1944 and the Humberside Aircraft Preservation Society recovered it in 1983.

Halesworth (Holton) (Station 365)

Description: American fighter base.
Location: Built in the village of Holton between the A144 and B1124 roads about two miles north-east of the market town of Halesworth.
Directions: from Holton take the B1124 and continue on up the hill and turn sharp left into minor road where the auxiliary fuel tank soon comes into view.
Comments: On an unclassified road off the B1124 is a polished marble stone with a plan view of the runways and perimeter track and an 8th Air Force badge dedicated to the 489th Bomb Group. Further along the road on a grassy bank in front of some wartime buildings is mounted an aircraft drop tank. Painted on it are the words: 'USAAF Station 305, Halesworth, 95th Air Wing, 8th Air Force. 56th Fighter Group July 1943–April 1944. 489th BG May

1944–Nov 1944. 5th ERS Jan 1945–May 1945. 496th FTG March–May 1945.' Three aircraft are also painted on the tank, representing units based here. Most of the runways and perimeter track are used as a turkey farm, with large sheds on the runways. The Halesworth Memorial Association was formed in late 1996 with the ambition of opening a museum dedicated to the 56th Fighter Group. After being given an original building on the old USAAF Command site by the owner, Mr John Cliff, work was soon in progress and the museum was opened in August 1997. The Museum is open April–October, Sundays and Bank Holidays 2.00pm–5.00pm. Refreshments, Museum Shop, Rest Room. Admission is free. If you see the flags flying they are open.

About a mile and a half from the memorials is the Triple Plea pub, which was a favourite with the Americans at Halesworth. Inside is USAAF memorabilia, including photographs and a 'Photos-in-Pubs' picture. *(See also, Ashby)*

Honington (Station 375)
Description: RAF and American fighter base.
Location: In north-west Suffolk seven miles from Bury St. Edmunds.
Directions: Taking the B1106 make for RAF Honington sign at roundabout and carry on through Fornham All saints to A134 then turn left. RAF Honington is about 5 miles further along.

Honington airfield in August 2006. (Author)

175

Passing Honington airfield in an AAC Lynx in September 1996. (Author)

Comments: Now the station for the RAF Regiment; outside the Guardroom is a dwarf brick wall on which are plaques honouring the 364th Fighter Group and just outside the main gate is a second memorial, bearing the inscription: 'Eighth Air Force USAAF. In memory of the men of the 1st Strategic Air Depot RAF Honington AAF595 1942–1946. Never forgotten, forever honoured. Dedicated 26 September 1987.'

Horsham St. Faith (Norwich) (Station 123)
Description: RAF and 8th Air Force base used by the 56th Fighter Group and 458th Bomb Group. Now Norwich International Airport.
Location: On the A140 northbound Norwich to Cromer road.
Directions: Follow the road signs to Norwich Airport from the city centre and ring road.
Comments: The Royal Air Force left Horsham on 24 March 1967 and during the following two years, the major part of the airfield and buildings were sold to Norwich City and County Council, the airfield in turn becoming Norwich Airport and an Industrial Trading Estate. *(see also City of Norwich Aviation Museum)*

Horsham St. Faith (now Norwich Airport), in June 1997 with the Officers' Mess (bottom right). (Author)

Horsham St. Faith (now Norwich Airport), in August 1999. (Author)

The Officers' Mess at Horsham St. Faith (now Norwich Airport) now demolished. (Author)

Ketteringham Hall (Station 147), Norfolk

Description: 2nd Bomb / Air Division Headquarters December 1943–June 1945.

Location: On unclassified road 3 miles E of Wymondham, 7½ miles SW of Norwich near to Hethel airfield.

Directions: Follow the A11 and then left to Ketteringham village church.

Comments: in WWII Ketteringham Hall, once the headquarters of Team Lotus, the international Formula 1 motor racing team was the Headquarters of the Second Air Division, Eighth Air Force and its fourteen Bombardment and five Fighter Groups (4th, 56th, 355th, 361st and 479th). A plaque on the wall commemorates 'the brave American men and women who served in World War II from 1942 to 1945, and the 6,300 men who lost their lives, whose names are listed on the Roll of Honor in the American Memorial Room of the Norwich Central Library.'(The Forum, Millennium Plain, Norwich, Norfolk, NR2 1AW. Reception desk & enquiries. Tel: 01603 774747. Trust Librarians office. Tel: 01603 774748. Fax: 01603 774749. *email address:* 2admemorial.lib@norfolk.gov.uk *web site address:* www.2ndair.org.uk)

Ketteringham Hall, Norfolk, the former 2nd Air Division HQ. (Author)

King's Cliffe (Station 367)

Description: American fighter base.

Location: Twelve miles west of Peterborough and 1½ miles NE of the village of King's Cliffe.

Directions: Go into Wansford and continue on minor road for King's Cliffe airfield.

Comments: the RAF watch office still stands, the hangars have been dismantled and most of the runways and perimeter removed for farming. Four miles NE of village on the boundary of the former airfield is a memorial incorporating vertical representations of a Spitfire and Mustang wing and the twin booms of a P-38 Lightning. The badges of the RAF and USAAF squadrons based at Kings Cliffe are engraved on the plinths and an inscription reads: 'King's Cliffe airfield, Station 167. To commemorate the eternal memory of those American, British, Belgian and Commonwealth airmen who gave their lives in the cause of freedom 1939 1945. Lest we forget.' It was unveiled by the Duke of Gloucester on 10 December 1986.

Leiston (Theberton) (Station 373)
Description: American fighter base.
Location: On unclassified road 13 miles NW of town.
Directions: Turn right from Old Post Office and turn right on to B1122. Immediately after level crossing turn left into West End road. Go straight on to the Cakes and Ale caravan site where there is a fine model of a P-51 Mustang.
Comments: On the site of the wartime airfield is a stone in memory of the 357th Fighter Group, 'The Yoxford Boys'. Flying Mustangs, they were based here from November 1943 to July 1945.
On a corner wall of the old Post Office building in Leiston is a bronze plaque commemorating the 357th, dedicated on 8 May 1980. Its inscription reads: 'United States Air Force Eighth Fighter Command 357th Fighter Group. Dedicated to the brave men who made the supreme sacrifice in the fight for freedom 1944–1945.' Sixty-nine names are listed underneath.

Little Walden (Hadstock) (Station 165)
Description: American fighter base.
Location: Off the B 1052 Saffron Walden road, 13 miles N of village and three miles north of Saffron Walden in what was formerly Little Walden Park.
Directions: Turn onto A604 for Linton then turn right on to B1052 and go through Hadstock. Hangar at right, control tower at left.
Comments: In the restored control tower is a plaque commemorating the men of the 409th Bombardment Group (L). Photographs of aircrew and Mustangs flank a plaque for the 361st Fighter Group. The operations block is now a garage.

Madingley, Cambridgeshire
Description: Cambridge American Cemetery.
Location: Approximately 3 miles W of Cambridge on the A1303.
Comments: This imposing cemetery and memorial, which covers 30 acres was constructed on behalf of the American Battle Monuments Commission in 1956 and is dedicated to

the lives of the US service personnel who perished whilst serving in the UK during World War II. At the entrance is the Visitors Building and a flagpole 72ft high, the base of which is inscribed with the quotation: '*To you from failing hands* we *threw the torch – be yours to hold it high'*. Running parallel with the A1303 are the Tablets of the Missing. A limestone wall extending 472 feet from the Visitors Building to the Memorial Building is inscribed with the names of 5,126 United States personnel who died or went missing on active service. At the western end of the wall is the Memorial Building, which is divided into a chapel and a museum showing the progress of the war between 1942 and 1945. The 3,811 headstones in the cemetery are arranged in a fan of seven curved rows, all set within carefully maintained lawns. The cemetery is open daily between 8.00am and 6.00pm, April to September 8.00am to 5.00pm October to March and limited parking is available outside the main entrance. Tel: 01954 201350.

Martlesham Heath (Station 369)
Description: RAF and American fighter base.
Location: South of the A12 trunk road 3 miles north of Ipswich.
Directions: Control tower and Douglas Bader pub are on left side of the A12 down a road from roundabaout to the new village.
Comments: On the former RAF parade ground, which was unveiled on 13 June 1946, is a memorial to the seventy-two US airmen lost whilst flying from here. Their names are listed, with the dedication: 'In grateful memory of the members of .the 356th Fighter Group USAAF from this station who gave their lives during the war 1939 to 1945. This plaque is erected by their British friends to commemorate the stay of the USAAF at Martlesham Heath.'

On 6 December 1984 Mr. Peter Claydon of the Martlesham Heath Aviation Society Control Tower Museum presented a framed photograph of Colonel Philip E. Tukey's P-51 Mustang to the Black Tiles Restaurant and public house. Colonel Tukey was CO of the 356th Fighter Group at Martlesham Heath, 24 April–3 November 1944 and 11 January–October 1945. The photograph is on display in the bar.

Martlesham Heath control tower in October 2002 when 356th Fighter Group veterans were treated to a flying display by aircraft including two Stearman biplanes. (Author)

The memorial to the seventy-two US airmen lost whilst flying from Martlesham Heath, which was unveiled on 13 June 1946. (Author)

The mural of St. Francis of Assissi at Kesgrave near Martlesham Heath airfield. (Author)

The control tower has been refurbished by members of the Martlesham Heath Aviation Society and is open from the first Sunday in April until the last Sunday in October 2pm–4.30pm. Admission is free.

At Kesgrave nearby (see signs for Hall's gravel pit) a pump house bears a mural of St. Francis of Assissi, painted by an American airman named Smith who was based at Martlesham Heath. It was painted for the widow of Squadron Leader Rope in 1944. *(See also Playford)*

Metfield (Station 366), Suffolk
Description: American base used by the 353rd Fighter Group and the 491st Bomb Group in WW2.
Location: Six miles SE of Metfield village off the B1123. Harleston to Halesworth road.

Directions: Follow the B1123 to Metfield and the airfield is close by the village of the same name.

Comments: Very little remains of this desolate airfield.

Mount Farm (Station 234)

Description: American PR/fighter base.

Location: In the Thames valley three miles north of Dorchester at Drayton St Leonard.

Directions: Leave junction 7 on M40 motorway and head SW on the A329 to Stadhampton. Turn right on to B480 to Chislehampton, then left on to B4015 and go to A423. Turn left and go about a mile to the Berinsfield roundabout. Turn left into minor road and left again. Memorial and St Mary and St Berin church are on the right.

Comments: Inside the church is a Roll of Honour and a memorial/visitors book. Across the A423 at Dorchester Abbey is the American Garden. There is a small plaque for the 7th PG(R) mounted on a fragment of runway concrete laid at the edge of a flower bed. *(See Berinsfield, Oxfordshire)*

Nuthampstead (Station 131)

Description: American fighter and bomber base used by the 55th Fighter Group and the 398th Bomb Group in WW2.

Location: Three miles west of the A10 Hertford to Royston trunk road.

Directions: Leave the M11 motorway at Junction 8 at Bishops Stortford and head west on A120, then onto A10 towards Royston to Barkway. Sign for minor road at right to Nuthampstead.

Comments: There is a memorial to the 398th Bomb Group and a memorial seat.

Playford

Description: Playford Hall: a moated Elizabethan mansion, with 18th century alterations, that was owned by the Marquis of Bristol. It served as the billet for personnel from Martlesham Heath airfield. Thomas Clarkson, prominent in achieving the abolition of slavery, died in the Hall in 1846, aged 85. It is believed that the house stands on the site of the home of the eminent 15th century knight, Sir George Felbrigg. In the garden area and by a tree is the site of the grave of 'Jeep' a coyote mascot of the 360th Fighter Squadron.

Location: West of Woodbridge and four miles from Ipswich.

Directions: Follow A12 towards Woodbridge and turn left on minor road to the village.

Comments: John 'Wild Bill' Crump, a pilot in the 360th Fighter Squadron, 356th Fighter Group at Martlesham Heath who was billeted at Playford Hall, had a coyote called 'Jeep' who flew five fighter missions with him in a P-47 Thunderbolt fighter. 'Jeep' was only two weeks old when Crump acquired him from a Nebraska farmer. He accompanied his master to Baton Rouge, LA, where Crump qualified as a fighter pilot and 'Jeep' was given his GI immunisations and military papers. To bypass Britain's strict rabies laws 'Jeep' travelled in a gas mask case aboard the *Queen Elizabeth*. Crump recalls:

> Halfway across, a colonel came to my quarters to inquire if I actually had a coyote aboard. I couldn't deny it since 'Jeep' was snoozing on my bunk. He came from Oklahoma and knew about coyotes, but he saw how tame 'Jeep' was and didn't show any concern – maybe because there were no live chickens on the ship. 'Jeep' became a favourite of the squadron and became especially friendly with the squadron cooks.

'Jeep' flew his five combat missions in September 1944 during Operation 'Market Garden', in which approximately 350 US AAC fighters bombed and strafed targets in the Netherlands in support of Allied airborne landings. On one mission Crump came under attack and when he threw his Thunderbolt around the sky in a successful evasive action, the negative G-force kept a frightened, wide-eyed 'Jeep' floating around the cockpit until Crump anchored him to a convenient handle. On 24 November 1944 'Jeep' was killed when ironically, he was run over by a four-wheeled jeep. 'Jeep' was buried with full military honours under a tree in front of Playford Mill, an impressive Elizabethan mansion and an Eagle Squadron billet. A bugler sounded taps and a 'missing man formation' thundered overhead with a low altitude victory roll by Crump. 'Jeep' is the only member of the species Canis latrans known to have served in combat in WWII. After his death, Crump flew with no other mascot. There was a plate over 'Jeep's' grave but in 1991 Crump returned with a special plaque, which was put on the grave, under the large tree. It simply reads, 'In memory of Jeep N.M.I.' (In the US Forces, N.M.I. is No Middle Initial).

Raydon (Station 157)
Description: American fighter base.
Location: On the B1070.
Directions: Take the Raydon-Hintlesham road, which crosses part of the old airfield east of the village.
Comments: In St. Mary's church on the B1070 the vestry doors bear the 8th Air Force emblem and the words: 'In remembrance of the men of the 353rd Fighter Group USA 8th Air Force who served in Raydon 1944–1945 and in remembrance of their return visit on the 25th August 1984'.

At **Nayland** the name of 2nd Lieutenant Charles F. Gumm of the 354th Fighter Group USAAF is inscribed on the village war memorial. On 1 March 1944 his Mustang P-51B 43-12410 suffered engine failure just after taking off from Boxted. Remaining with his aircraft 2nd Lieutenant Gumm cleared the village but he was killed when the aircraft hit a tree and crashed.

Saffron Walden, Essex
Description: Site of a USAAF Memorial and Wing HQ in WWII.
Location: Three and a half miles west of Royston.
Directions: Follow M11 and turn off onto B1039 or B1383. The Anglo-American Memorial Playing Fields are near Bridge End Gardens in the town centre.
Comments: The 65th Fighter Wing Memorial Apse or 'Anglo-American Memorial', as it is known, is 'In honoured memory of the officers and men of the 65th Fighter Wing of the United States Air Force and the men and women of the Borough of Saffron Walden who gave their lives in the defence of freedom 1939–1945.' It is set in a rose garden and was dedicated in 1955. The names of the casualties are listed on stone tablets for all groups in the wing.

Steeple Morden (Station 122)

Description: American fighter base.

Location: 3½ miles west of Royston.

Directions: From Royston leave the A505 onto the minor road to Litlington. Turn left towards Steeple Morden. Airfield and memorial are on the left.

Comments: Three Nissen huts, which were the 'Ready room' and associated buildings for the 358th Fighter Squadron remain in good condition. Nearby, on a plot at the side of the minor road between Litlington and Steeple Morden is the superb 355th Fighter Group memorial, made of Portland and York stone with a Mustang propeller forming an impressive centrepoint. The 355th's achievements are described thus: 'Memorial, 355th Fighter Group and Support Units USAAF 8th Air Force. Activated Orlando FL 12 November 42. Arrived UK 6 Jul 43. First combat mission 14 Sep 43. Last combat mission 25 Apr 45. Over 1500 E/A damaged-destroyed. Distinguished Unit Citation 5 Apr 44. Over 2,000 American airmen served here. Dedicated 12 May 1981.'

On farmland on the left between the memorial and Litlington is a brick building which was air-conditioned during the war, when it was used for planning missions. Nearer the road is a lone hut,

The superb memorial at Steeple Morden in 1997. (Mike Fuenfer)

187

The beautiful stained glass window at St. Catherines, Litlington. (Author)

which was a machine-gun workshop. The memorial bears the badges of the 355th's three squadrons, the Second Air Scouting Force and the group crest. Inscribed are outlines of the Thunderbolt and Mustang and details of the group's units and war record, with 'over 1,500 enemy aircraft damaged – destroyed'. In front of the memorial is a part of a large granite block from a blitzed church in London, inscribed '355th Fighter Group. AAF Station 122. Steeple Morden. July 1943–July 1945'. When the runways were laid, rubble from blitzed buildings in London was used for the perimeter track and the granite block on the memorial had been used in a false fireplace in the control tower.

On Sunday 16 May 1993, the 50th anniversary of the 355th's arrival at Steeple Morden, the Bishop of Huntingdon dedicated a memorial stained glass window to the 355th Fighter Group in St. Catherine's Church, Litlington. John F. Dobbertin Jr's design shows the American eagle, wings spread over the blazing red and yellow emblem of the 355th Fighter Group with a glistening dagger streaking through the centre and there are silhouettes of the P-51 Mustang and P-47 Thunderbolt. At the top of the centre window is the 8th Air Force emblem. Fifty 355th Fighter Group veterans attended the dedication. Twelve years later, in May 2005 only three of the veterans made it back to Steeple Morden for the VE-Plus 60 years celebration in the church, which was covered by the BBC.

Thetford, Norfolk
Description: Site of USAAF memorial.
Location: Town centre.
Directions: On the old A11 off the bypass.
Comments: Under the statue of Thomas Paine opposite the main entrance to the Bell Hotel is a plaque with side elevations of three P-51 Mustangs in the respective colours of the 368th, 369th and 370th Squadrons of the 359th Fighter Group. On a blue background are the words: 'Presented to the people of Thetford and East Wretham a memorial honouring those men of the 359th Fighter Group who gave their lives and also those who served during World War II, 67th Fighter Wing US 8th AF, East Wretham-Great Hockham Airfield 133, 1943–1945. Dedicated 3rd August 1985.'

Wattisham (Station 377)

Description: RAF and American fighter base.

Location: Nine miles north-west of Ipswich.

Directions: Off the B1078, 6 miles south of Needham Market.

Comments: A plaque unveiled in the Briefing Room in Station HQ in October 1988 commemorates the 479th Fighter Group, the final fighter unit to be assigned to the 8th Air Force. The Group. known as 'Riddle's Raiders' after their CO, Colonel Kyle L. Riddle, was based here from May 1944 to November 1945.

The Wattisham Airfield Station Historical Collection was opened in November 1991. It is housed in the original Station Chapel, which was built by the USAAF in 1943. The collection includes an extensive photographic record, depicting the history of the Station from initial preparation and construction in 1937, up to the present day. Other exhibits include a fine display of models, artifacts and memorabilia. The museum is open every Sunday April–October 1400–1630. All other times by appointment only. Tel: 01449 728307 / 678189.

Westhampnett (Station 352) West Sussex

Description: RAF and American fighter base.

Location: On unclassified road 2 miles NNE of Chichester.

Directions: At Milford join A286 and go through Haselmere, Midhurst and Singleton. Immediately after Singleton, turn sharp left at signpost for Downlands Museum and Goodwood Race Centre. Go through the park, past Goodwood House (on left). Aerodrome is on right.

Comments: The old control tower is now used as offices and the wartime perimeter track, which was a motor racing and car testing circuit during 1948–66, is still used as a motor circuit while light aircraft and helicopters operate from the grass airfield. On 26 September 1987 the veterans of the 31st Fighter Group unveiled and dedicated a memorial at the edge of the airfield near the smaller, modern control tower. The memorial is made of white Portland stone and ebony black granite and has the inscription: 'To the members of 31st Fighter Group who from this aerodrome on 26th July 1942 joined their British Comrades in Combat, as the first United States Fighter Group in the European theatre.'

Pen & Sword Books have over 1500 titles in print covering all aspects of military history on land, sea and air. If you would like to receive more information and special offers on your preferred interests from time to time along with our standard catalogue, please complete your areas of interest below and return this card (no stamp required in the UK). Alternatively, register online at www.pen-and-sword.co.uk. Thank you.

PLEASE NOTE: We do not sell data information to any third party companies

Mr/Mrs/Ms/Other.............. Name..

Address..

.... Postcode........................

Email address...
If you wish to receive our email newsletter, please tick here ☐

PLEASE SELECT YOUR AREAS OF INTEREST

Ancient History	☐	Medieval History	☐	English Civil War ☐
Napoleonic	☐	Pre World War One	☐	World War One ☐
World War Two	☐	Post World War Two	☐	Falklands ☐
Aviation	☐	Maritime	☐	Battlefield Guides ☐
Regimental History	☐	Military Reference	☐	Military Biography ☐

Website: www.pen-and-sword.co.uk • Email: enquiries@pen-and-sword.co.uk
Telephone: 01226 734555 • Fax: 01226 734438

Pen & Sword Books
FREEPOST SF5
47 Church Street
BARNSLEY
South Yorkshire
S70 2BR

2

*If posting
from outside
of the UK
please affix
stamp here*

Westhampnett airfield. (Richard E. Flagg)

At the Goodwood Park Hotel nearby is a 'Photos-in-Pubs' picture, showing a 31st Fighter Group Spitfire at Westhampnett.

Wormingford (Station 159)

Description: American fighter base.
Location: Five miles NW of Colchester to the west of the A133 Colchester-Bures road.
Directions: One mile south-east of the village.
Comments: A memorial honours the 150 casualties of the 362nd Fighter Group and there is a simple plaque to the 362nd over the door of what was once a guard hut.

Wormingford airfield in June 2006. (Author)

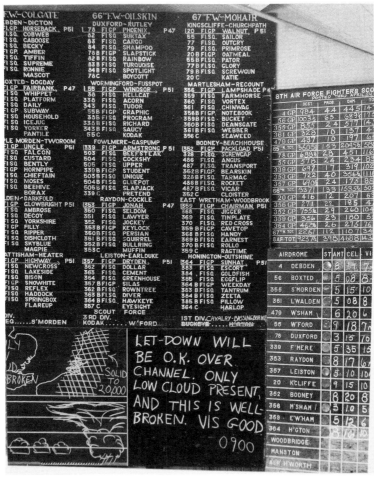

Mission summary showing 65th, 66th and 67th Fighter Wing Operations.
(USAF)

APPENDIX 2

8th Air Force Fighter Command Order of Battle

67th FIGHTER WING
Walcot Hall, Near Stamford

Group	Squadron / Markings	Base	Aircraft
20th Fighter Group. 8 black, 7 white vertical stripes aft of spinner. November 1944	55 (KI) 77 (LC) 79 (MC) Squadron identification symbols on fin and rudder adapted from end of 1943 55 (triangle) 77 (circle) 79 (square)	King's Cliffe, Northants 26.8.43–11.10.45	P-38H&J/P-51C/D&K
352nd Fighter Group Medium blue spinner and 36-inch bottom cowling band swept up on side panels to aft of exhaust stubs and up to cockpit. Whole upper panel blue April 1944.	328 (PE) 486 (PZ). 487 (HO). From December 1944 rudder colours 328 (red) 486 (yellow) 487 (blue)	Bodney, Norfolk 8.7.43–7.2.45	P-47D/P-51B/C/D&K
356th Fighter Group Red cowling panels with horizontal lines of blue diamonds.	359 (OC) 360 (PI) 361 (QI) From December 1944, rudder colours: 359 (yellow) 360 (red) 361 (blue) Also spinners from February 1945.	Goxhill, Lincs 27.8.43–5.10.43 Martlesham Heath, Suffolk 5.10.43–2.11.45	P-47D/P-51D&K
359th Fighter Group Bright green spinner and side and bottom cowling panels.	368 (CV) 369 (IV) 370 (CR & CS) From November 1944, rudder colours. 368 (yellow) 369 (red) 370 (dark blue)	East Wretham, Norfolk. 19.10.43–2.11.45	P-47D/P-51B/C/D&K

364th Fighter Group White spinner, 12-inch blue and white band aft of spinner.	383 (N2) 384 (SY) 385 (SE) Replaced by symbols on vertical tail 383 (circle) 384 (square) 385 (triangle)	Honington, Suffolk 10.2.44–3.11.45	P-38J/P-51D
364th GP Scouting Force.	385th a/c. Red outline to tail, red spinner 12-inch cowling band in white. No triangle on tail; only a/c letter in black.	Honington, Suffolk	P-38J/P-51D

65th FIGHTER WING
Dane Bradbury Private School, Saffron Walden

4th Fighter Group Red spinner. 24-inch red cowling band swept back and down. January 1945	334 (XR) 335 (AV) 336 (MD) Spitfires only. 334 (QP) 335 (WD) 336 (VF) on P-47s and P-51s.	Debden, Essex. (Satellite, Gt. Sampford) 29.9.42–27.7.45 Steeple Morden, Cambs 20–27.7.45–4.11.45	Spitfire V/P-47C&D/P-51B/D&K
56th Fighter Group Red 24-inch cowling band. March 1944	61 (HV) 62 (LM) 63 (UN)	King's Cliffe, Northants 13.1.43–5.4.43 Horsham St. Faith, Norfolk 5.4.43–8.7.43 Halesworth, Suffolk 8.7.43–18.4.44 Boxted, Essex 18.4.44–9.9.45 Little Walden, Essex 9.9.45–10.10.45	P-47C/D&M

355th Fighter Group P-47s. White propeller boss and 12-inch cowling band. P-51s. White spinner and 12-inch cowling band in squadron colour.	354 (WR) 357 (OS) 358 (YE) Rudder colours from November 1944. 354 (red) 357 (blue) 358 (yellow)	Steeple Morden, Cambs 8.7.43–3.7.45	P-47D/P-51B/C/D&K
361st Fighter Group Yellow spinner. 36-inch yellow band swept up and aft from bottom cowling panel to front of cockpit.	374 (B7) 375 (E2) 376 (E9) Rudder colours from November 1944 374 (red) 375 (medium blue) 376 (yellow)	Bottisham, Cambs 30.11.43–26.9.44 Little Walden, Essex 26.9.44–4.2.45 (St. Dizier, France 25.12.44–15.2.45 (air Echelon only) Little Walden 9.4.45–3.11.45	P-47D/P-51B/C/D/K
479th Fighter Group No Group colour	434 (L2) 435 (J2) 436 (9B) Rudder colours from August 1944 434 (red) 435 (yellow) 436 (none)	Wattisham, Suffolk 15.5.44–22.11.45	P-38J/P-51D
355th GP Scouting Force	354th a/c. Black bar above WR code. Upper half of cowling band in bright green.	Steeple Morden, Cambs	P-47D/P-51B/D/K

66th FIGHTER WING
Sawston Hall near Cambridge

55th Fighter Group Green, yellow, green spinner.12-inch green and yellow cheque band round cowling aft of spinner	38 (CG) 338 (CL) 343 (CY) Symbols on vertical tail surfaces from end of December 1943 38 (Triangle) 338 (Circle) 343 (Square)	Nuthampstead, Herts 16.9.43–16.4.44 Wormingford. Essex 16.4.44–21.7.45	P-38H & J/P-51D&K
78th Fighter Group Black and white checks on cowling	82 (MX) 83 (EL) 84 (WZ) From November 1944, rudder colours: 82 (red) 83 (white) 84 (black)	Goxhill, Lincs 1.12.42–3.4.43 Duxford, Cambs 3.4.43–10.10.45	P-38G/P-47C&D/ P-51D&K
339th Fighter Group White, red, white. spinner 12-inch red and white cheque band round cowling aft of spinner	503 (D7) 504 (SQ) 505 (6N). From November 1944, rudder colours: 503 (red) 504 (green) 505 (yellow)	Fowlmere, Cambs 5.4.44–10.10.45	P-51B/C/D/K

353rd Fighter Group Black, yellow, black, yellow spinner. 48-inch black and yellow cheque band round cowling to end of exhaust stubs.	350 (LH) 351 (YJ) 352 (SX) From November 1944 Squadron colours: 350 (yellow) 352 (black) 351 (none)	Goxhill, Lincs 7.6.43–3.8.43 Metfield, Suffolk 3.8.43–12.4.44 Raydon, Suffolk 12.4.44–10.10.45	P-47D/P-51D&K
357th Fighter Group Red, yellow, red Spinner. 12-inch red and yellow cheque band round cowling aft of spinner.	362 (G4) 363 (B6) 364 (CS) From November 1944, rudder colours 362 (none) 363 (red) 364 (yellow)	Raydon, Suffolk 30.11.43–31.1.44 Leiston, Suffolk 31.1.44–8.7.45	P-51B/C/D/K
55th GP Scouting Force	338th a/c. From late 1944 red and white checks on rudder	Wormingford, Essex.	P-38H&J/P-51D&K

APPENDIX 3

Leading Aces

Leading USAAF Aces in the ETO 1942–45 (Air-to-Air Victories)

Ace	Units	Total Score
Colonel Francis S. Gabreski	56th Fighter Group	28
Colonel Robert S. Johnson	56th Fighter Group	27
Major George F. Preddy	352nd Fighter Group	26.83
Colonel John C. Meyer	352nd Fighter Group	24
Colonel David C. Schilling	56th Fighter Group	22.5
Captain Fred J. Christensen	56th Fighter Group	21.5
Captain Ray S. Wetmore	359th Fighter Group	21.25
Colonel Walker M. Mahurin	56th Fighter Group	20.75
Captain Donald S. Gentile	4th Fighter Group	19.83
Colonel Glenn E. Duncan	353rd Fighter Group	19.5
Captain Leonard K. Carson	357th Fighter Group	18.5
Major Walter C. Beckham	353rd Fighter Group	18
Major Boleslaw M. Gladych	56th Fighter Group	18
Lieutenant Colonel Hubert Zemke	56th/479th Fighter Group	17.75
Major John B. England	357th Fighter Group	17.5
Captain Duane W. Beeson	4th Fighter Group	17.333
1st Lieutenant John F. Thomell	352nd Fighter Group	17.25
Captain John T. Godfrey	4th Fighter Group	16.33
Major Gerald W. Johnson	56th Fighter Group	16.5
Major William T. Whisner Jr	352nd Fighter Group	15.5
Captain Richard A. Peterson	357th Fighter Group	15.5
Major Robert W. Foy	357th Fighter Group	15
2nd Lieutenant Ralph K. Hofer	4th Fighter Group	15

Bibliography

Arbib Robert S. Jr., *Here We Are Together, The Notebook of an American Soldier in Britain* (1944)

Beaty, David, *Light Perpetual: Aviators' Memorial Windows* (Airlife 1995)

Blue, Alan G., *The Yoxford Boys*

Bowman Martin W. *8th Air Force At War* (PSL 1994)

Bowman Martin W. *Echoes of East Anglia* (Halsgrove Publishing Ltd 2006)

Bowman Martin W. *Great American Air Battles* (Airlife 1994)

Bowman Martin W. *USAAF Handbook 1939–1945* (Sutton 1997, 2003)

Bowman Martin W. *Ghost Airfields of East Anglia* (Halsgrove Publishing Ltd 2007)

Bowyer, Michael J. F. *Action Stations 1: East Anglia* (PSL) 1990

Caldwell, Donald, *The JG 26 War Diary Vol. 2.* Grub Street, London. 1998.

Congdon, Philip *Behind the Hangar Doors* (Sonik)

Cora Paul B., *Yellowjackets! The 361st Fighter Group in World War II* (Schiffer 2002)

Delve, Ken, *The Military Airfields of East Anglia Norfolk and Suffolk* (Crowood 2005)

Dobbertin, John F. Jr., *The Window at St. Catherine's* (Universe Inc. 2005)

Duxford Diary 1942–45 (W. Heffer & Sons 1945)

Fox, George H., *8th Air Force remembered: An Illustrated Guide to the memorials, memorabilia and main airfields of the US 8th Air Force in England in WW2* (ISO Publications 1991)

Fry, Garry L. *Eagles of Duxford: The 78th Fighter Group in World War II* (Phalanx Publishing 1991)

Gotts, Steve, *Little Friends: A Pictorial History of the 361st Fighter Group in WW2* (Taylor Publishing 1993)

Hale, Edwin R. W. and Turner, John Frayn, *The Yanks Are Coming* (Midas Books 1983)

Hall, Grover C., *One Thousand Destroyed* (Morgan Aviation Books Dallas 1946)

Height, Andy, *Airfield Focus 1: Duxford* (GMS 1992)

Hewitt, Lieutenant Colonel R. A. 'Dick', *Target of Opportunity: Tales & Contrails of the Second World War* (Privately Published November 2000)

Keillor, Pete, *Wandering Through World War II* (Privately Published 2003)

Fairfield, Terry A., *The 479th Fighter Group in WW2 in Action over Europe with the P-38 & P-51.* (Schiffer 2004)

Fairhead, Huby & Tuffen, Roy, *Airfields & Airstrips of Norfolk & Suffolk* (Norfolk & Suffolk Aviation Museum)

Fairhead, Huby, *Aeronautical Memorials of Suffolk* (Norfolk & Suffolk Aviation Museum 1989)

Fairhead, Huby, *Aeronautical Memorials of Norfolk* (Norfolk & Suffolk Aviation Museum 1995)

Francis, Paul, *Military Airfield Architecture From Airships to the Jet Age* (PSL) 1996

Freeman, Roger A., *Airfields of the Eighth Then and Now* (After the Battle) 1978

Freeman, Roger A., *Mighty Eighth War Manual* (Jane's 1984)

Freeman, Roger A., *The Mighty Eighth* (MacDonald 1970)

Freeman, Roger A. *The Mighty Eighth In Art* (Arms & Armour 1996)

Freeman, Roger A., *The Mighty Eighth in Colour* (Arms & Armour 1991)

Innes, Graham Buchan, *British Airfield Buildings Expansion & inter-War Periods* (Midland 2000)

Innes, Graham Buchan, *British Airfield Buildings of the Second World War* (Midland 1995)

Lande D. A., *From Somewhere in England* (Airlife 1991)

Marriott, Leo, *British Military Airfields Then & Now* (Ian Allan Publishing 1997)

McLachlan, Ian, *Final Flights* (PSL 1989)

McLachlan, Ian, *USAAF Fighter Stories* (Sparkford. Haynes Publishing, 1997)

McLachlan, Ian, *USAAF Fighter Stories; A New Selection* (Sutton Publishing 2005)

Nelson, Larry, *Historic Tales of the Wild Blue Yonder* (Privately Published 2006)

Olynyk, Frank, *Stars & Bars: A Tribute to the American Fighter Ace 1920– 1973* (Grub Street 1995)

Powell, R. H., *The Blue Nosed Bastards of Bodney* (Privately Published Dallas 1990)

Raby, Alister *The Battle of Britain Then and Now* (After The Battle 1980).

Russell, Ernest E., *A Mississippi Fighter Pilot In WWII* (Trafford Publishing (UK) Ltd 2008)

Scutts, Jerry, *Mustang Aces of the Eighth Air Force* (Osprey 1994)

Smith David J., *Britain's Memorials & Mementoes* (PSL 1992)

Spick, Mike, *Luftwaffe Fighter Aces* (Ivy Books 1996)

Speer, Frank E., *The Debden Warbirds: The 4th Fighter Group in WWII* (Schiffer, 1999)

Walker, Peter M., *Norfolk Military Airfields* (Privately published 1997)

Wells, Ken, *Steeple Morden Strafers 1943–45* (East Anglian Books 1994)

Wolf Dr. William, *Victory Roll! The American Fighter Pilots and Aircraft in WWII* (Schiffer 2001)